MANAGING
FACTORY
MAINTENANCE

Managing
Factory
Maintenance

Joel Levitt

Industrial Press Inc.

Library of Congress Cataloging in Publication Data

Levitt, Joel, 1952–

    Managing factory maintenance / by Joel Levitt. — 1st ed.

       304 p. 15.6 × 23.5 cm.

    Includes index.

    ISBN 0–8311–3063–6

    1. Plant maintenance—Management.   I. Title.

TS192.L47   1995

  658.2—dc20   95–40897

                                                                 CIP

INDUSTRIAL PRESS INC.
200 Madison Avenue
New York, New York 10016-4078

FIRST EDITION
First Printing
Managing Factory Maintenance

10   9   8   7   6   5   4   3   2   1

Dedication

To my father, Semond Levitt, who introduced me to the world of factories and production.

Contents

Figures

Preface

Sometime in the 1990's, maintenance as we knew it died. Strategies and tactics practiced for a lifetime no longer worked. These old paradigms are now being reevaluated in light of the new corporate order.

With this in mind, we must ask fundamental structural questions about what types of tasks maintenance personnel should perform, and who should carry out these tasks. The first question of this inquiry is "what is the mission of maintenance?"

What is the mission of maintenance? There once were as many different answers to this question as there were companies. If there was a mission statement, it probably mentioned quick reaction times in fixing breakdowns, or improving service to the customer. Other popular ideals included reducing downtime, or improving cost control or quality. A few identified safety or environmental security. All of these missions were good, useful, and important, but each ignored the deeper issue—culture has changed and maintenance has been forced to change with it. There is something very simple that transcends these older missions or values.

What happened to our organizations? What is the best way to organize to manufacture automobiles, to generate electricity, or to provide medical care? Increasingly, the answer is not a traditional structure with rigid departmental boundaries. The optimum structure is more often a matrix, network, or another form previously unimagined. In some notable cases (such as movie making), the best organization is virtual: one that is organized ad hoc for a specific project or product. Independent specialist contractors who are experts in their fields are assigned the various functions. The team dissolves when the task is completed, changed, or terminated. The "lean and mean" virtual corporation is far less dependent on bricks and mortar (and maintenance). It is more likely to rely on a contractor than an in-house department.

Even in conventional company structures, each employee is expected to add value to the product. Everyone who does not is expendable or outsourceable. Traditional in-house activities such as data processing, order fulfillment, and even product manufacture are often being outsourced. In the past, improved maintenance practices meant adding people. No more! Imagine the reaction of a current corporate hero, a tough cost cutter renowned for engineering a 1000-employee right sizing effort, when you attempt to justify additional staff to carry out a PM system.

There is a conflict between the old mission statements and the new culture. Those mission statements must be wrong because they conflict with the new core corporate philosophy of being a lean, mean, fast, and in-your-face competitor. The old vision of maintenance is as obsolete as a relay rack.

The maintenance department's new mission is:

"to provide excellent support for its customers by reducing and eventually eliminating the need for maintenance services."

Traditional roles and responsibilities must be redefined to accomplish the new mission. On one hand, maintenance and machining and tooling design must merge to integrate maintainability improvements into design in order to take advantage of the accumulated knowledge of both groups. On the other hand, routine maintenance activity should be merged into operations. The TPM model illustrates that the entire maintenance effort will benefit from operator involvement.

In the new maintenance organization, breakdowns are not okay! There is a traditional attitude on the part of maintenance that breakdowns are to be expected (after all, that's what we are paid for!). The same defective attitude supports designs that demand constant investment in the form of PM and routine maintenance. The acceptance of the status quo is intolerable and should be unacceptable in the new maintenance. A breakdown should be viewed with shame as a failure of the system. Any equipment requiring periodic attention to avoid breakdowns is likewise a failure of design engineering.

Where do PM and predictive maintenance fit into the new structure? PM is now one strategy among many to reduce breakdowns. It is a way station on the road to maintenance improvements. PM is the best tool to use until you can get to the problem and eliminate it for good.

How does the new maintenance operate on a day-to-day basis? Without continuous improvement in the delivery of maintenance, there is stagnation and complacency. What seems like a secure situation gives way to an eventual upheaval when management realizes that maintenance is not keeping pace.

What steps can be taken to keep the orgaization secure? What is at stake is the survival of your organization. Active participation in continuous improvement is the only antidote to the constant pressure of competition. Continuous improvement requires everyone's imput because the knowledge needed must be spread throughout the organization. The impact of maintenance decisions spans all of the functions of an organization. Ongoing maintenance improvements result in increased productivity, improved competitive position, lower cost to deliver product or service, and increased stature for maintenance professionals.

MANAGING
FACTORY
MAINTENANCE

1.
World Class Maintenance Management

Maintenance is a Service Business

Maintenance is a business. In every business, staying close to the customer helps ensure survival and allows the business to thrive. Traditionally, the mission of maintenance has been to support the productive output or activity of the organization. That was accomplished by a single-minded focus on the machines, systems, and buildings (called assets). This paradigm is best stated by the dictionary definition of maintenance management, which is "the act of directing the preservation of assets."

There is a new view in organizations—a new paradigm for the whole business that refocuses on the process and the people rather than the product. This new view has caused a revolutionary shift in the mission of maintenance.

The new paradigm of business is to focus on streamlining, and reducing the inputs, to make the process of manufacturing more responsive. As a result, the mission of maintenance must conform to the continuous improvement of all processes of the manufacturer. The new mission includes the idea that *the maintenance department should work endlessly to reduce and, where possible, eliminate the need for maintenance.* This activity has suppliers, processes, and customers.

The new mission serves both classes of customers powerfully (they are denoted by the capital and lowercase "C"). The big "C" is the ultimate customer who is outside the organization—the sale of the product to the Customer creates an invoice which results in a payment which pays our salary. The other customers are internal to the organization, such as production, finishing, assembly, administration, warehousing, etc. Most maintenance departments spend all their energy thinking in terms of the internal customers and ignore the needs of the Customers external to the company.

Any activity that has an impact on the ultimate Customer—such as breakdowns, downtime, quality variation, or missed delivery—is critical and has to be looked at very closely. To constantly improve the delivery of maintenance service, we need outside resources. Successful maintenance departments build long-term partnership-type relationships with outside vendors. They rely on these vendors to be experts in their fields. When chosen carefully, treated well, and allowed to make a profit, these vendors multiply our ability to respond quickly and inexpensively to our customer's needs.

One large manufacturer chose 21 vendors in different commodity classes for all maintenance purchases. If it needed an odd ball bearing that the approved power transmission vendor didn't have, the vendor would do the research, negotiate the best price and terms, and buy it. The deal called for a management fee paid to the vendor with incentives rather than a markup. The vendor also supplied local stocking of parts, fast dropoff service, engineering, and a host of other services.

This book focuses on the process of maintenance in the middle of the diagram shown in Fig. 1. The processes of maintenance (to a great extent) determine the outcome of the maintenance service. The process starts with the customer's communication with the

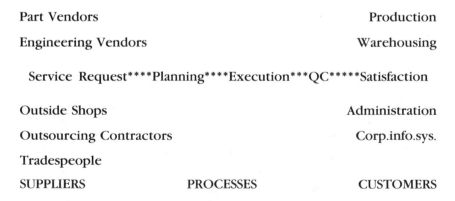

Part Vendors   Production

Engineering Vendors   Warehousing

Service Request****Planning****Execution***QC*****Satisfaction

Outside Shops   Administration

Outsourcing Contractors   Corp.info.sys.

Tradespeople

SUPPLIERS   PROCESSES   CUSTOMERS

Fig. 1. Maintenance is a process with suppliers and customers.

maintenance department. It also starts when a PM task list is due or when an inspector sees a problem and submits it for future correction. The process continues with the planning function, material ordering, prioritization, scheduling, and execution. The process is also responsible for communicating with the customer that the job is complete (or is being held up by parts, etc.).

A bad process depends on the individual heroism of maintenance management, support staff, and technicians to serve the customer; for example, the stores group is a vendor to the maintenance process. If a part that should have been in stock is not in stock, then service to the customer suffers, excessive downtime might result, and a delivery window might be missed. Individual heroism such as digging through the dumpster and remachining a discarded part to fit might be the only way to serve the customer. Good service with a defective process is the exception, and is only the result of special effort.

On the other hand, a good process provides good service with only occasional acts of heroism. High quality lies at the core of the process. Improvements in the quality of maintenance delivered envelope the entire process from improved supplier relationships, to improved work order handling, to better understanding of true customer needs—today and tomorrow.

In production maintenance, improvements in maintenance quality equal lower cost, because when you improve quality, then costs decrease from less waste, rework, maintenance requirements, downtime, variation, etc., which improves productivity while reducing disruption.

Quality in maintenance makes the organization more competitive and allows it to capture a greater market share with better quality and lower cost (the greater margins allow you to become the lowest cost producer). As an added bonus to you and your staff, the company gets to stay in business while providing stable jobs.

Attributes of World Class Maintenance

The wave of organizational changes required to run a comprehensive quality program has hit the maintenance department. Consistent quality depends directly on the maintenance department. Maintenance professionals the world over have heroically struggled against inadequate support, old equipment, inadequate engineering, little time to test processes, excessive runtime between services to provide uptime, high tolerances, and uninterrupted utilities. This wave of change is great news for maintenance. Maintenance wisdom has long been ignored. Maybe, now, the maintenance department will get the respect it deserves and support it needs.

Competitiveness in world markets—and survival—now drives the changes in how top management views maintenance. A world class maintenance department enhances the organization's ability to provide their product or service. The maintenance department becomes a strategic asset of the organization rather than a "necessary evil."

The following 20 attributes are derived from the author's visits to many maintenance facilities, and from the excellent work of W. E. Deming, Don Nyman, and others. For additional discussion of some of these steps, see Chapter 12.

1. Top management has awareness and appreciation of the significance of maintenance to the overall objectives of the organization.

The first key to a world class maintenance effort is the support, understanding, and trust of top management. These factors are frequently missing. One mission of the world class maintenance department is education of top management. While much of maintenance is unknowable (the exact minute a gear will crack), much of maintenance reality (machines *do* break down if they cannot be serviced) can be taught. Only a short-sighted executive would ignore the dire warnings of their finance vice president. Yet many managers routinely ignore the warnings, knowledge, and experience of their maintenance managers.

Consider the following example. A power utility builds a generating station in the Midwest with the design specification that it will be able to have 85–95% availability. To support this level of availability, the designers have long and detailed meetings with the maintenance leadership. Every failure mode is discussed, looked at, planned for, and (where possible) designed out. The capital spares inventory was 24 million dollars (just reduced by the maintenance department to 15 million). This utility realizes that profit in power generation hinges on the wisdom of the maintenance input to the design and operation of the plant. This is an example of support, appreciation, and understanding of the role of maintenance to the success of the operation.

2. Have a mission statement.

A mission statement is necessary to run a world class maintenance department. The mission statement becomes the primary benchmark that the staff can use for effective decision making. The mission statement covers the issues of customer orientation, continuous improvement, quality, safety, environmental position, employee development, downtime, proactive stance, and any industry-specific areas.

In the executive conference room of a vehicle manufacturer, there was a beautiful poster titled "Mission Statement of the Corporation." This poster cost in excess of $5000 to produce and print. I asked a class full of maintenance supervisors sitting in the room at the time, "Does the company have a written mission statement?" At least half said "no," and the others thought they did. No one in the room could remember any of the statements of the documents. This is an example of a bogus mission statement, since it will not guide anyone toward better quality, safety, or anything.

The mission statement defines the organization in concrete terms. This is particularly useful for tradespeople in the middle of the night, far from the other workers, or for one new to the company when there is no supervisor to ask. The mission statement answers the questions of how much effort should be put into quality, safety, etc.

In organizations that are serious about their mission, everyone knows the critical items on the mission statement. If you doubt this, ask a Dupont employee about safety, or a Saturn employee about product quality.

3. Maintain a constancy of purpose (emphasize long-term goals and views).

There is nothing more debilitating to the effectiveness of a maintenance department than the management "flavor-of-the-month club;" that is, a management that jumps on the bandwagon of every new guru and loses the focus necessary for world class performance. Last year it was empowerment, this year it's stay close to the customer, and next year we will worship at the alter of quality.

The march of equipment and facility deterioration moves at a slow, inexorable pace. This can be eased by good lubrication, cleaning, and bolting practices. The effects of the deterioration can be treated by corrective maintenance. The results of decay can be foreseen by predictive maintenance techniques. But no technique can stop the march.

Upgrading a reactive department to preventive, then to predictive, then to World Class is usually a six-year effort. Great achievements like world class maintenance require a long-term commitment. This attitude should be reflected in a long-term budget. A five- or even ten-year budget for maintenance and rehabilitation is needed. This will provide information to the corporation regarding future needs. Many of the assets that maintenance supports have long decay cycles; these long cycles respond best to a constant approach, where we look, record, and document the deterioration for years while planning an intervention. The intervention is then well conceived, reasoned, planned, investigated, and executed.

4. Both maintenance and management should have patience.

Going hand in hand with constancy of purpose is patience. Maintenance problems take a long time to develop, and consequently they take a long time to fix. Substantial maintenance system and procedure improvements require time and investment. Initial results often take a year or more. Managers used to dealing with monthly results will be uncomfortable with the longer time spans.

Steven Covey, a leading business thinker, speaker, and consultant, sums up the paradox in saying that there must be an unchangeable core at the center of the organization to be able to react quickly and effectively to the marketplace. This core consists of the essential values that make the organization successful in the marketplace. While the marketplace makes different demands on a month-to-month basis, the core values stay the same.

One of the core values is the way we treat the people and assets under our stewardship. That value is the organization's attitude toward maintenance and maintenance leadership. Patience is also an expression of trust.

5. Focus on service to the customer.

Another core value of the organization is excellent service to all the customers. The maintenance department is a service vendor for all other departments of the organization. These departments are the customers, and they need to be understood through regular communication, periodic surveys, and needs assessment. When maintenance efforts fail, it is the customer who suffers. Every member of the maintenance work group should be familiar with the impact of their actions on the customer.

No maintenance department (of the over three thousand that have attended the author's classes) has ever gotten bad feedback from attending to the customer too well. Maintenance brainpower would be well spent if it concentrated on faster delivery of higher levels of service. The maintenance department must strive to serve the real needs of the customer.

Some effort would be rewarded in determining what maintenance changes could impact the outside Customer. How can what you do impact them and their business? How can you make your outside customer's life easier? It is hard to see what you can do to help the outside customer beyond doing your job inside, but the rewards for success are great. Any substantive improvements will enhance the competitive position of your whole organization.

Many maintenance organizations take a superior attitude toward production (the customer). They say, "we are the real brains, and production is a bunch of idiots." They can prove it by showing you all of the stupid things that happen in production. These departments miss the fundamental point that our purpose flows from service to the customer. Maintenance leadership misses opportunities to coach maintenance workers that their attitude impacts the level of service.

6. Be proactive, not reactive.

The world class maintenance department does not allow critical assets to deteriorate to the point of a breakdown. The proactive maintenance department does not wait for the breakdown, but goes out onto the plant floor looking for impending problems. Implicit in the proactive approach is the will to take equipment out of service for repair before the breakdown. The reactive approach says, "don't fix it if it ain't broke." The proactive approach says, "don't let it break down—period!"

Examples of proactivity include inspection, cleaning, tightening, lubrication (all PM activity), complete testing of new equipment, operator certification programs, continuous training programs, well-thought-out storerooms, reviewing designs before construction for maintainability, etc.—in fact, all activity related to avoiding break-down in the future.

Consider the attitude of a program to preserve assets in an art museum. Of course, an art museum has a great restoration depart-ment after damage has been done. The bulk of their activity, how-ever, is in creating an atmosphere that will prevent deterioration in the first place. Maintenance departments need to get in front of the action, out on the shop floor, and not wait for bad things to happen.

There is another aspect to proactivity: a proactive maintenance department will spend a significant percentage of its assets on main-tenance prevention. The most proactive stance of all is to eliminate the need for maintenance.

The toughest aspect of proactivity is self-discipline. You must maintain your proactive activity without feedback and support. In fact, proactivity requires doing things that may seem irrational to outsiders without a long explanation.

7. Implement root cause analysis.

Getting to the root cause and fixing it is the best way for a main-tenance department to gradually improve the delivery of mainte-nance service to the customer. Root cause treatment comes in two stages.

First, most good mechanics will work on a breakdown until they understand and repair the root cause. This distinguishes the real me-chanic from the parts changer. Root cause analysis requires some time to study a system. Many organizations imagine that they do not have the time, and so they force premature decisions on the mechanic. I say "imagine" because they seem to have the time to repair the problem over and over again.

The second stage is to reengineer the system to avoid that mode of breakdown in the future. This may be well beyond most mechanics on complex systems. In production-facilities competition, service requirements and the sheer cost of maintenance require this level of expertise.

Root cause analysis can be done by anyone who has knowledge about the actual situation, and ideas about elimination of the problem. Root cause investigations are an excellent area for using the team concept and breaking down interdepartmental barriers (building teams with maintenance mechanics, engineers, customers, etc.).

Root cause analysis is a proactive skill; it requires attention to equipment history, engineering, and the details of the failure. The mechanic who successfully undertakes this analysis has the ultimate cross-training experience.

8. Operate under a team concept.

Many maintenance problems today are too complex to be solved by a single person. World class maintenance departments recognize and capitalize on the different skills and expertise of different members of their crews and other departments. Teams are used extensively to solve problems, plan jobs, and institute improvements. A single maintenance worker might be involved in several teams simultaneously. Some teams might be ad hoc (set up for one problem) and others might be standing teams (for safety, environmental, etc.). Leadership training and opportunities to safely exercise leadership are part of the team concept.

One of the most interesting examples of team projects was in the automotive industry. Automobile companies routinely buy competitor's products and disassemble them. In one company, they put together a volunteer, ad hoc (one time, as required) team consisting of design engineers, people from general assembly, maintenance people, and even administrative people. This team would take the car apart and attach the parts to boards for display. They would analyze the part counts, assemble techniques, and prepare a report and presentation for the larger new-car staff. It was considered a fun assignment.

9. Phase out traditional interdepartmental barriers.

Significant amounts of expertise needed for successful maintenance are hidden away in other departments in the organization. The world class maintenance department taps into these storehouses of expertise by breaking down interdepartmental barriers. Traditional departments that support maintenance (engineering, stores, safety, purchasing, housekeeping) are actively involved in maintenance issues. Nontraditional departments (finance, cost accounting, data processing, marketing, strategic planning) are also brought into the maintenance decision processes. The team idea includes interdepartmental teams with significant input from the different departments. For world class maintenance to take hold and flourish, detailed maintenance knowledge must cross departmental boundaries.

Part of the goal of phasing out these barriers is the distribution of maintenance knowledge throughout the whole organization. Unfortunately, under old departmental structures, maintenance knowledge was not well distributed throughout the organization. The result was ill-advised decisions such as the oil refinery mothball project. When the oil prices fell, an oil company decided to mothball one of their refineries. The accounting department estimated that the savings would be $10 to $15 million per year. They further estimated that the refinery would cost $75 to $100 million to put back on line. To maximize the savings, they laid off the entire maintenance staff and just had security personnel on the site. After 8 years, the price of oil recovered to the point that they wanted the refinery back for some large contracts. Because of a lack of basic maintenance knowledge and a lack of effective communication, the refinery was almost a complete loss and cost almost $700 million to bring back. Maintenance knowledge would have alerted accounting that a small investment of $2 to $3 million per year would have preserved the plant. Eight years without investment caused significant deterioration. Of course, the return on investment would have been $16 to $24 million lower.

The rest of the effort in phasing out barriers is directed toward bringing sophisticated cost accounting, finance, engineering, and other skills to the maintenance department.

10. Allow customer participation in maintenance (with training!).

World class maintenance requires the operator's involvement. The more the operator is involved, the better for all concerned. The benefit for the operator is the feeling of being the owner of the process/machine, improved responsibility, and higher total productivity. The operator is the logical person to perform basic PM tasks because he/she is in daily contact with the machine—the machine is really theirs.

The benefit for the company is improved tracking of responsibility, improved quality, and improved knowledge, which leads to improved productivity. A knowledgeable operator who feels responsible will make better parts at a higher rate. Downtime will be reduced, and small problems will be addressed quickly.

If we did all of the PM's we should do, we would rapidly find there is more maintenance to do than maintenance has people to do it. We need an additional resource. The largest hidden resource of the maintenance department to service the assets is the users themselves. In some industries (such as the trucker checking his/her own oil and doing the pretrip inspection), it is commonplace for operators to participate in the preventive maintenance procedures. In fact, the pretrip inspection is the *law* in trucking and aviation. In other industries, operators don't touch the equipment; the operator just pushes the button or watches a gauge.

This ownership takes another step in some departments where the operator acts as a helper on large repairs, or as a safety watch person if confined space entry is required. Once properly trained, the operator can be a great asset. In factories, the best implementation of this idea is called TPM (Total Productive Maintenance, see Chapter 8).

11. Implement cross training (also known as multiskilling).

High levels of productivity require some level of cross training. Cross training simplifies job planning. Less time is lost coordinating different crafts. Many maintenance departments have enough people but have inadequate staffing (in particular, crafts or skills). Cross training also provides a more secure job because of the possibility of changing to jobs where the craft is more scarce when the times are slack.

The major reasons for cross training are to improve productivity and to allow one person to do more of the job so he/she can feel ownership. A powerful motivator of the maintenance worker is the feeling of pride in a job well done. A cross-trained worker is more likely to feel pride because he/she did the whole job.

Multiskilling depends heavily on a successful training and testing program. In all multicraft shops, training is an initial issue. Many firms bring in outsiders, tech schools, or other training professionals to organize the massive training effort. Some of the best maintenance departments pay the craftspeople for qualifications in extra crafts.

Consider the following. In an aluminum mill in northern Alabama, there are 11 crafts in the maintenance shop. In a worst case scenario it could take 4 people and their supervisors to change a small motor. We would call out the pipe fitters (if we needed to disassemble or change the piping), sheet metal mechanics (for modifications to the shroud or cover), an electrician to remove the wires, and the trusty mill wright to remove and replace the motor. While the quality of each craft would be great, the productivity would be well below world class standards.

12. Provide continual training.

Your factory has increasingly sophisticated technology. The technology is 1980's through 1990's vintages. Your crew was last in formal training 15, 20, 25 years ago. This gap must be filled by updating skills through continual training. The alternative is lower and lower quality, increased downtime, and an increasingly complete inability to perform even routine root failure analysis.

You and your staff are involved in continual training. This is an investment that organizations make in their major assets (people). Training has three steps (if followed, they give the most results for the least training dollars): 1) analyze the job for needed knowledge, skills, and attitudes; 2) evaluate the candidate for training against the job's requirements; 3) develop a training prescription. Traditional "shotgun" approaches are too expensive. The training process does not stop.

In a new automaker's plant, the standard for training is 96 hours per year for all workers. A high-tech manufacturer in the upper Midwest requires 5% (104 hours) of all direct hours be spent in class of some type. These firms realize that this investment pays interest in the ability of the craftspeople to adapt to new technology, new processes, and new organizational structures. Topics could include engineering, craft skills, multicraft skills, computerization, maintenance management, safety, or your own industrial process.

13. Share information.

Information essential for effective maintenance exists in many locations in the organization. Maintenance touches many different levels of activity. Each level has important information. Some examples of critical information that impacts maintenance decision making are fixed asset accounting methods/decisions, overhead costs, downtime costs, equipment retirement cycles/budgets, interdepartmental priorities, etc. World class maintenance can happen only in the atmosphere of open exchange of financial and production data.

Without critical information, the maintenance department is out of the loop and cannot make effective decisions. Worse than being out of the loop, maintenance can make good maintenance decisions that work against the organization.

For example, in a plastic extrusion plant in Maryland, a maintenance worker found a problem with an extruder by using the latest predictive maintenance technology. Immediate repair to prevent breakdown would cost $500; after breakdown, the bill would have jumped to $5000. He was very proud because the savings was estimated at $4500. He discussed the plan with the shift manager and the maintenance manager, and they decided to do the repair immediately on second shift and go for the savings. The next day, the manager walked into the Wednesday morning production/maintenance scheduling meeting. He was greeted by a chilly silence before the meeting. Production had missed a just-in-time delivery for a new customer that morning. They asked, "did he know why unit 5 was taken off line for an entire shift and a half?" Almost $40,000,000 of new business was put at risk. Lack of information (lack of communications) created a costly blunder.

14. Use benchmarking.

The benchmark was the mark old world craftspeople made in their benches, used for measurement. All parts made were compared to the benchmark to assure they would fit. Today, a benchmark is the standard for performance as well as a means of measurement. We use benchmarks to tell if an operation is improving, stagnating, or declining. A world class department wants to know how it is doing.

One of the problems of maintenance has been the difficulty in finding benchmarks that effectively measure the performance of a maintenance department. Some measures that can be effective would be number of completed work orders versus number of incoming work orders, PM hours to total maintenance hours, percentage and quantity of emergency work, number of callbacks, downtime (or uptime, include downtime reason), production quantity/quality, maintenance cost per product shipped, and many others.

There are three ways to compare the benchmarks for maintenance. The first is the traditional historic internal benchmark. This takes a common measure (such as downtime, time to respond, number of work orders issued, maintenance cost per revenue dollar) and compares this year to historical numbers. The historic benchmark is the most widespread and most widely understood. Usually, three years of comparisons by quarter is most useful.

The second benchmark is called best-in-class. This benchmark looks outside your plant and compares your maintenance department against the best in your industry. You have to study your competitors and look for the best maintenance department in your industry and compare yourself to them. This information may be available from trade journals or associations. The benchmarks are so critical to some organizations that they spend a $100,000 or more to have unbiased outsiders collect these data. Organizations with several plants of the same type will create their own best-in-class benchmark.

The third type of benchmark is the best-in-the-world. This is very hard to do well. You compare yourself function by function to the best in any industry. One function might be handling customer complaints. Compare yourself to the best customer complaint handlers in the world such as Federal Express or Lands' End (catalog retailer).

15. Make continuous improvements.

There are many factors that contribute to an organization's survival, and one of the main ones is continuous improvement. Continuous improvement is everyone's job. The world class challenge is to produce the same or greater output at a higher quality with fewer inputs. One of the inputs is maintenance effort and parts. You should establish the inputs needed per unit of output (output is measured as cars assembled, cases of soda bottled, barrels of oil refined, etc.). Through your ongoing continuous improvement processes, the input per unit output should drop. Last year's numbers can be the benchmarks to beat for this year.

Continuous improvement is also an attitude. Many maintenance people fall into a dangerous rut when they feel satisfied that a system is understood and its failure mode is familiar. They feel as if they can handle anything that might happen. While it is nice to feel as if you can handle anything that might happen, it is deadly to accept the status quo. You have to fight this tendency to maintain the attitude of continuous improvement.

16. Make people, rather than technology or computer systems, the priority.

We run the risk of thinking that if only we had a new computer, bar coding with a new scanner, or other tool, our maintenance department would finally get better. The truth is that most good maintenance practices are basic and low tech. Having our everyday people (our first-line maintenance workers) do the basics well is critical to manage breakdown. Our *people* are the important asset. Our thoughts toward improvement should look to their needs first. Any system changeover should consider good employee treatment, adequate adjustment period, and sufficient training.

We routinely see systems that have run amok. In one case, a system spit out PM tickets for equipment retired a decade ago. There seemed to be no one left to change (or want to change) the file to get rid of the irrelevant PM. In addition, the PM tickets in question had to be closed out as complete, or all of the reporting would be off. In another case, the maintenance manager got a 1400-page weekly maintenance report. It included everything for all divisions mixed together. Data processing could never suppress the extra information.

17. Consider people first so that every other option is looked at before layoffs (W. E. Deming says, "drive out fear").

Many organizations lay off people as a first resort rather than a last resort. Mindless expansion and contraction of the permanent workforce is immoral in today's competitive world. Every other option should be tried before layoffs, including shortening work weeks; slashing executive salaries; using maintenance for construction work; offering accelerated retirement; and transferring maintenance to production, staff, and even marketing jobs. Companies need new strategies to cope with expansion, contraction, plant closings, and changes in the product mix.

It is quickly becoming clear that the true asset of a manufacturer is the know-how of the employees. This specific knowledge is essential in all aspects of modern management. Processes cannot be improved, products cannot be made more consistently, and benchmarks cannot be achieved without specific knowledge. This knowledge comes from years of solving problems in a factory or an industry.

In all theories of motivation, when a person's paycheck is threatened, he/she is not available to perform the highest quality work. It is difficult to concentrate on the details that create quality and safety in an anxiety-producing environment.

18. Be willing to run controlled experiments.

Controlled experimentation is the key to new knowledge. Using the Shewhart cycle or other technique, ideas are introduced by the workforce, tested, refined, and retested. Root cause analysis (determining the root cause, and how can we fix it) will also suggest need for experimentation. Controlled experiments support continuous improvement.

Every maintenance budget should have some money set aside for maintenance experiments. A good starting figure might be 1% – 2% of the regular budget. Returns on investment should be tracked, and successes should be publicized.

The only way to improve is to try different ideas, technologies, techniques, approaches, etc. Coupling experimentation with job enhancement and training will propel your maintenance department to the forefront of its field.

19. Apply statistical tools to maintenance.

In the great move toward quality in the late 70's and 80's, production and top management discovered some old statistical tools. These tools explained the problem of natural variation. They also would help identify when a process went out of control. Maintenance can learn from statistical thinking with failure analysis, PM intervals, replacement life, and other areas.

The excellent reliability record of the commercial aviation industry is due, in large part, to the application of statistical tools to aircraft reliability. Much credit for reliability goes to the aircraft companies, component suppliers, and engine manufacturers. The actions that really keep the planes up—even after 20 or 25 years— are the scheduled replacements, inspections, and the tremendous database kept by the FAA.

Statistical techniques are only as good as the database they are derived from and the reliability of the intervention. The database includes information, maintenance records, and utilization data on all of the commercial aircraft in the U.S. Reliability is based on millions (or billions) of miles, and on hundreds of thousands of takeoff/landing cycles.

Part of basic training for maintenance apprentices should be calculation of Mean Time Between Failures (MTBF), standard deviations, and how and when to use them. PM systems would improve overnight if we got rid of "emotion-driven" PM intervals.

20. Promote self-motivation.

A self-motivated workforce is the result of management doing hundreds of little things right. The principles of world class maintenance will result in a self-motivated workforce and an environment that is exciting to work in.

There are great opportunities for organizations that put major effort into making products, understanding the real maintenance issues, and becoming experts in their activities. 1990 begins the decade of expertise. The marketplace will no longer tolerate amateur manufacturers, governmental institutions, hospitals, or any other institution.

2.
Evaluate Your Maintenance Department

Maintenance Fitness Questionnaire

Instructions: Circle the number of the item that your plant needs to improve upon. Put a star in front of the questions that you think are of vital interest to your organization.

A. Initiation and Authorization of Work

1. Is a written work order, on a printed form, used for all jobs?

2. Is a written work order in place prior to starting a job for all work except genuine emergency repairs?

3. Are regular meetings held between users and maintenance to set priorities?

4. Is there a reasonable "date wanted, time wanted" space on each work order, with restrictions against ASAP, RUSH, HOT?

5. Is all work performed classified for repair reason, such as corrective, routine, breakdown, PM, diagnostics, construction, PCR (Planned Component Replacement), and modernization?

6. When statistical process control limits are exceeded, is a maintenance request initiated?

7. Is a single person or unit responsible for screening work orders?

8. Is there a designated group of maintenance users with authority and training to request maintenance work?

9. Are restrictions more severe for approval of special jobs as opposed to normal repairs?

(In the author's opinion, items 1, 2, 7, 8, and 9, rank 1–5 in importance, respectively.)

B. Systems and Procedures

1. Do all maintainable units (machines, buildings, systems, etc.) have unique ID numbers?

2. Are maintenance managers part of the top-level strategic planning for the future of the facility, product, or organization? Are maintenance managers taken seriously?

3. Is there an absolute commitment on a long-term basis to improve the quality and reduce the cost of maintenance among all top management and maintenance management people?

4. Are there written procedures for the work order system that are reviewed and followed?

5. Is an up-to-date lockout and confined space procedure attached to all appropriate PM, emergency, and corrective work orders? (Attachment to the units themselves is o.k.)

6. Are there up-to-date MSDS sheets available, used, and understood by maintenance workers?

7. Do all work orders have the ID numbers (asset number) of the unit worked upon?

8. Are all work orders costed: labor hours × mechanic chargeout rate and parts used for a total cost per work order.

9. Is there a written, understandable hazardous waste policy with procedures that ensure compliance with the law and responsible handling of the wastes?

10. Are there any unnecessary systems, reports, and procedures left over from when the organization was bigger or when reporting requirements were different?

11. Are systems in place that detect craftsperson-induced problems? Is the percentage of rework or callback less than 3%?

12. Do your systems highlight when overtime is below or above predetermined setpoints, such as 3%–9%?

(In the author's opinion, items 1, 4, 8, and 10 rank 1–4 in importance, respectively.)

C. CMMS (Computerized Maintenance Management Systems) Information Systems

1. Do mechanics and supervisors have the training, knowledge, positive attitude, and access into the Maintenance Information System to investigate a problem?

2. Are useless and faked data kept out of the system, and are the data coming out of the system commonly held by management and the workers to be accurate and useful?

3. Can the system give answers to most maintenance questions without the services of a programmer?

4. Is repair history from the date in service immediately available with enough accuracy to detect repeat repairs, trends, and new problems?

5. Can the system generate meaningful comparison data between like machines, buildings, and cost centers?

6. Can the system isolate the "bad actors" using the Pareto principle or exception reporting to identify the problem machines, craftspeople, or parts? (Usually this is done with exception reporting.)

7. Are the printed reports set up to give each level of management only the level of detail they can reasonably use with more detail available on demand? Are one-page management

reports showing critical operating ratios with trends available?

8. Is the CMMS system supported by either a responsive vendor or a responsive data processing department?

9. Is the CMMS system integrated with stores, purchasing, payroll, CAD/engineering?

10. Are new capabilities being added to the system regularly?

11. Can the system look at component life and provide an analysis for MTBF (mean time between failure)?

(In the author's opinion, items 1, 4, 8, and 10 rank 1–4 in importance, respectively.)

D. Preventive/Predictive/Conditioned-Based Maintenance

1. Does top management support the PM system with their attention and money?

2. Is the reduction and eventual elimination of maintenance requirements a mission of the maintenance department?

3. When deficiencies are found during inspection, are they written up as scheduled work and completed in a reasonable time? Will production control or production give up a machine if a potential problem is detected during the PM inspection and maintenance wants to schedule a repair?

4. Do repeated or expensive failures automatically trigger an investigation to find the root cause and correct it?

5. Are the operators/users trained to do routine maintenance and PM where possible? Is there an extensive operator training program to avoid common problems?

6. Was there an economic analysis of each item on the task list proving ROI (Return on Investment)? Does each item relate to a failure mode that is either expensive, dangerous, or common?

7. Is Planned Component Replacement (PCR) considered when equipment is mission critical or has high downtime costs?

8. Are high-technology inspections used such as vibration analysis, ultrasonics, etc.?

9. Are the high-tech inspections integrated into and driven by the master PM schedule?

10. Will operations, production, or users allow the maintenance department to schedule downtime for PM?

11. Are units kept out of the PM system because they are in very bad shape or PM is not economically indicated? Was there an analysis of PM feasibility or was it just assumed that PM is the best alternative?

12. Does the actual failure history impact the frequency, depth, and items on the task list?

13. Are lube routes established? Do the lube people report abnormal machine conditions (and are they trained to do so)?

14. Is auto lube equipment in use or under real consideration?

15. Is the PM system driven by measures of equipment usage such as machine hour, energy, cycles, pieces, tons, etc.?

16. Are there multiple levels of PM on the same machine such as "A level" every 30 days and "B level" every year?

17. Are the task lists divided by interruptive, noninterruptive, and skill level?

(In the author's opinion, items 1, 4, 7, 13, and 16 rank 1–5 in importance, respectively.)

E. Planning, Scheduling, and Followup

1. Is the maintenance master schedule reviewed and updated at least weekly, and signed off on by operations management and other interested parties?

2. Does the operations department set realistic priorities for work orders they generate, taking into account maintenance department staffing, skills, etc.?

3. Is PM or scheduled work routinely displaced by jobs with preferential treatment (lower priority, but need to be done) such as a new electrical outlet for a boss?

4. Are maintenance work orders prioritized in a rational way to ensure that the most critical units are worked on first?

5. Are jobs routinely completed on time, on budget, as planned?

6. Does the mechanic show up to do a repair or PM on time (per schedule) 95% of the time, and is the unit returned to service as planned on time 95% of the time?

7. Is there an up-to-date master plan for all major jobs with important dates, durations of subprojects, critical paths, and labor and craft requirements?

8. Is PM scheduled by user departments, such as production control, or is there a direct linkage between the master production schedule and the PM schedule?

9. Is there a day's work for each craftsperson planned and written on a public schedule (that everyone can see) at least a day ahead of time for 75% or more of the craftspeople?

10. Is there a craft time breakdown on all planned work prior to the accomplishment of the work?

(In the author's opinion, items 1, 2, 9, and 10 rank 1–4 in importance, respectively.)

F. Purchasing, Parts, and Stores

1. Is the store room well laid out, with adequate space, controlled access, shelving, bins, and drawer units?

2. Can a maintenance craftsperson get the right part in less than 10 minutes 95% of the time?

3. Are all parts used for maintenance purposes tied to a unit number through the work order?

4. Is there an ongoing effort to use vendors as long-term partners for stocking, engineering, and problem solving?

5. Is there a periodic review of high-turnover high-cost items for possible savings?

6. Is there a review of expensive slow-moving items to see if they belong in stock at all?

7. Does maintenance have a specialist(s) who routinely purchases maintenance parts?

8. Is there an adequate information system support to help easy lookup and investigation of unknown parts? Is there a cross reference to indicate all of the units that a specific part can be used on?

9. Are the relationships between maintenance, purchasing, and stores departments good?

10. Are there established reorder points, order quantity, and safety stocks based on logical reasoning (not on emotion)?

11. Is there an annual physical inventory and review of all parts for obsolescence, spoilage, quantity-on-hand, reorder point, lead time, and safety stock?

12. Does the accounting system have a capital spares category for expensive, long-lead time "insurance policy" parts?

13. When a unit is retired, are the special parts required for that unit removed from stock (scrapped, sold, reworked for use elsewhere)?

14. Does the store room get PM lists and corrective workorders early, in order to kit up the parts in advance?

(In the author's opinion, items 1, 3, 7, and 13 rank 1–4 in importance, respectively.)

G. Budgeting, Backlog, Maintenance Ratios, and Work Measurement

1. Is the budgeting process real (developed against the maintenance demand created by machines and facilities) or just some calculation against last year's budget with some padding (to be cut away by top management)?

2. Is the current budgeting process likely to serve the best overall long-term interests of the organization?

3. Is there a five- or ten-year strategic maintenance plan, including projected capital replacements, which is reviewed and updated at budget time by both maintenance and top managers?

4. Is the relationship between the amount of output (production quantity such as cases processed or tonnage shipped) and maintenance staffing well understood and used for budgeting?

5. Is uptime tracked and are trends calculated along with downtime reason? Is there a well-known cost of downtime by machine, process, or facility? Is a Pareto analysis of downtime made and acted upon?

6. Is there a maintenance improvement fund or a maintenance R & D account to pay for experiments to improve maintainability?

7. Is there recognition that good maintenance practice has a major impact on other budget line items such as energy and regulatory compliance?

8. Are the energy and capital replacement line items looked at along with maintenance line items at one time?

9. Are budget savings available for reinvestment into other cost-reduction programs?

10. Is the ratio of maintenance dollars to overall revenue dollars (or some other commonly used overall measure) tracked, and are trends kept for at least three years?

11. Do major pieces of equipment have individual repair/replace budgets?

12. Is the budget performance kept up-to-date by month, with adjustments as necessary?

13. Is the ratio between scheduled and nonscheduled work tracked, and are trends charted for at least three years?

14. Is there a standard time for all repetitive jobs, PM's, and routine work?

(In the author's opinion, items 1, 4, 9, and 13 rank 1–4 in importance respectively.)

H. Guaranteed Maintainability

1. Are drawings and specifications on all new machines, processes, and buildings reviewed by the maintenance department early enough in the process so that changes can be made without adverse impact to the whole project?

2. Are specifications for product, process, or buildings discussed with the maintenance department to see if they are in line with existing skills, parts stocked, and tools?

3. Are new technologies on machines and building systems discussed with maintenance so that they can procure training and test equipment both before and during installation or construction?

4. Do designers or equipment buyers make use of failure and cost histories to make better decisions?

(In the author's opinion, items 1–3 are most important.)

I. Training, Hiring, and Employee Development

1. Is 1–5% of a technician's direct hours spent in craft, multicraft, or other related training?

2. Is cross training a goal for the department to allow craftspeople to do the "whole" job and provide scheduling flexibility?

3. Is there a consistent process to identify and hire the best maintenance workers, with the final decision being made by the maintenance department?

4. Is training for continuous improvement of skills part of the mission of the department?

5. Has there been a recent assessment as to the technology and skill set required to maintain the machinery, equipment, process, and buildings, with a comparison to the average skill set of the employees in the maintenance department?

6. Is there ongoing training of maintenance users (operators) to improve their operation of the equipment, help them correct minor faults, and improve their powers of observation (to improve the quality and accuracy of the maintenance request)?

7. Is training tracked and reviewed by supervision, the craftsperson, and management at least yearly? Is a determination made of benefit or return on investment?

8. Is training for the maintenance department part of all new equipment acquisition contracts? Is there consideration of the issue of training 1, 3, and 5 years later when it is more likely that the machine will need service?

(In the author's opinion, items 1, 4, and 8 rank 1–3 in importance, respectively.)

3.
Communication and Delegation

Why study communications?

- Communication supports management objectives.
- Good communication is a skill that can be learned.
- You will feel better about yourself if you are a better communicator.
- You will be a more effective delegator, which will make you a more effective manager.
- Your *family* life will also benefit.
- It's fun.

Some of the things that good communication requires:

- self-discipline to pay attention to all of the details of the interchange;
- knowledge and skills of communications techniques;
- awareness of what is going on with the other person;
- reason to communicate;
- intention to communicate by all parties.

Remember that 70% of the message of a communication comes across nonverbal channels: voice tone, voice volume, body positioning, facial expression, animation, air space, eye contact, fluency, physical barriers, hand gestures, skin coloration, breathing patterns, etc.

Important Issue: Note cross-cultural/ethnic/sex/class communication barriers; when dealing with people from groups different than yours, beware of assumptions, stereotypes, golden-rule thinking, unintended meanings, different gestures, and different customs.

Maintenance is a multiethnic, multicultural, multiclass field. It is almost inevitable that a maintenance work group will be diverse. There are many excellent books that highlight the pitfalls of assuming that your communication style is appreciated or even understood by your co-workers. It is beyond the scope of this text to do more than recommend study of the topic.

Opportunities Can Arise from Problems in Communications

Your customers enter the maintenance sphere of influence via a work order, service request, or other less formal means. A sound system will ensure that the vital communication of what needs to be done is complete and accurate. It takes discipline (write everything down and ask all relevant questions), knowledge, and skill to translate what the customer is asking for into what is actually *needed* for maintenance. It also takes sensitivity to the unspoken condition of the other person, which may be a problem or an opportunity. Finally, you and the customer must have the intention of taking care of the problem.

Look at your work request system as a communication opportunity. Any time a mechanic does the wrong job at the wrong place to the wrong unit, there is an opportunity to look at the effectiveness of your work initiation system. Any time there is a wild goose chase—a mechanic is sent out with the wrong tools, or materials, or expectations—there is an opportunity to review the internal communication effort.

Most supervision effort has traditionally been oriented toward discovering the identity of the person who "screwed up" when a breakdown occurs in communication. Most of these breakdowns occur because some part of the communication system doesn't work. If you investigate the defect in the system that allows mistakes to happen, then you can improve the whole system.

The survey in Fig. 2 can help you determine your current level of communication skills.

Fig. 2.   Inventory of current communication skills.

Score:	5	4	3	2	1	0
I am:	Very strong	Strong	Good	Fair	Weak	Very weak

Answer the following questions as honestly as you can.

1. I am relaxed when I am communicating   _____
2. I look people in the eye while talking   _____
3. I lead the discussion   _____
4. I encourage the other person to speak rather than   _____
    giving my opinions
5. I seek (rather than give) information   _____
6. I tend to summarize discussions rather than   _____
    evaluate who was at fault
7. I ask open questions   _____
8. I let communication happen anywhere rather than   _____
    only in my office, at my convenience
9. I talk minimally to encourage the other person to   _____
    talk
10. I facilitate the person's chance to talk   _____
11. I reflect back on how the person must have felt   _____
12. I can catch subtle clues in a person's speech,   _____
    manner, or gestures
13. I can keep up with someone in a conversation   _____
14. I have good timing in communications   _____
15. I will clarify rather than confuse a person   _____
16. I keep communications on target   _____
17. I know what people are talking about   _____
18. I accept all people just the way they are   _____
19. I am aware of myself when communicating   _____
20. I express my feelings when communicating   _____
21. I stay on the topic at hand   _____
22. I am aware of information on the nonverbal   _____
    channels of communication
23. I can tolerate and use silence in communications   _____
24. I stick with a problem and help define it   _____
25. I am effective in working with people's problems   _____

26. I can operate at deep levels of analysis _____
27. I understand people _____
28. I can restate what people say to demonstrate my understanding of what is being communicated _____
29. I catch the essence of and can summarize a communication _____
30. I build a strong bridge of rapport _____
31. I provide a supportive environment for people _____
32. I trust people and they trust me _____

TOTAL SCORE: _____

How to Score Your Answers

A perfect, 100% communicator   160 points

This person should write a book on communications. A perfect communicator possesses great discipline, skill, and awareness. Their star will rise (or has risen) in most organizations.

An "A"-level communicator   140 points or more

Many top executives are superior communicators at this level. They got to the top because people will work for them and with them. Their ideas and visions were properly transmitted. More importantly, people felt listened to when they spoke to these high-level communicators.

A "B"-level communicator   125–139 points

This good score shows some need to improve, but also that great territory has been covered. A sharpening of skills to the elite level will take work and time. A "B"-level communicator will rise in his/her organization.

A "C"-level communicator   105–124 points

This is an average communicator. Much work has been done, but there is still much to be done. Choose an area and concentrate on it for a month or two; then choose a new area and concentrate on that. After a year, see if your scores don't improve substantially. With the improvement in skills may come more responsibility as supervisors see the results of the effort.

A "D"-level communicator   90–104 points

Face the fact, you have work to do. You could be a great engineer or electrician (or whatever), but your message will not get across. Others won't understand you, and won't feel understood by you. Your impact on the organization is minimized by your inability to get your vision and your point across. Many people in this situation are more comfortable with machines, drawings, and the technical aspects of the job. Follow the advice for "C," and expect significant gains in a short time.

An "F"-level communicator   89 points or less

You may need coaching in reading, test taking, or English; this may explain the low score. There is nowhere to go but up. Keep a positive outlook, and follow the advice given to "D."

Delegate to Thrive

"Supervisors are not paid for what they can do but for what they can control."[1]

In *Webster's New World College Dictionary,* delegation is defined: "to entrust (authority, power) to a person acting as one's agent or representative." The first ground rule of delegation is to entrust both the authority (power) and the responsibility.

The supervisor's job is to work through other people. One of the most difficult transitions is from worker (being paid for how well you work) to supervisor (being paid for how well you work through others). One of your main jobs is the development of the people that work for you. Delegation will help develop talent within your work group. The effect of some responsibility on people is amazing.

Many supervisors resist delegating work to their subordinates. Often the reason is that the supervisor is sure that the subordinate can't handle it or that he/she can do it better. Other fears might be:

- that the subordinate might mess it up and be a bad reflection on the supervisor

[1] Stated by Lee Minor, teaching *How to Supervise People* (offered by Fred Prior Seminars).

- loss of control

- feeling threatened by training a replacement

- looking bad because other people are doing the "actual" work

- feeling less needed (wanting to always be the center of attention)

- that delegation might reduce their position.

On the other side of the coin, the subordinate might resist the assignment because they feel as if they are being set up, they are already too busy, or they've learned it's safer to rely on the supervisor.

Dos and Don'ts of What to Delegate

Do Delegate	Don't Delegate
1. Routine Tasks	1. Personnel Tasks
2. Time-Consuming Jobs	2. Job Assignments
3. Skill Improvement Tasks	3. Disciplinary Actions

Letting People Make Mistakes

It has been said that experience is gained through mistakes. Whether you agree with this or not, people have to be allowed to make mistakes, fail, and show bad judgement. An employee who only relies on the good judgement of an experienced supervisor or leader (instead of themselves) stunts his/her growth opportunities.

Through delegation, the wise supervisor can create a safe environment for mistakes. As a supervisor, you become the sidelines coach. Allow enough emotional space for people to make their own decisions, which will help them to grow. Refrain from interfering (we already know you can do it better)—as long as they are not in danger (to themselves, you, large batches of product, etc.), let them learn, it will make them better employees. Consider a relief supervisor slot as a training ground for future supervisors when you vacation (or go to seminars).

The One Minute Manager

The One Minute Manager[2] is one of the most popular self-improvement books for managers and supervisors. The rules presented apply directly to maintenance leadership. We strongly encourage all maintenance managers, supervisors, and other leaders to purchase and read this excellent book. To maximize the effect of *The One Minute Manager* concepts, discuss the goals and concepts with your work group first. Encourage people to read the book (circulate some copies). Discuss the concepts so everyone knows what you are trying to accomplish. The authors of the book (particularly Ken Blanchard) have created an extensive library of books, tapes, and seminars to teach this and more recent material. The following three concepts are simple and powerful.

1. *One Minute Goal Setting:* In delegation most of the problems stem from the other person not really knowing the what, when, and how of your goal. Make it clear what they are to do. Have them write the goals (or scope of work) out on a single sheet of paper. The total statement should be less than 250 words. In the words of the author, "feedback is the breakfast of champions." The goals should be written in the first person (using "I") and in the present tense. They should read their goals every morning or whenever they start to work on the project (should take less than 1 minute). In simpler delegations, the goals might correspond to a scope of work.

2. *One Minute Praising:* Catch people doing something right! Look for *approximately* right. Remember that feedback is necessary for personal continuous improvement. This is a deeper request than it seems on the surface. This request goes against the training and culture of maintenance. Maintenance people have cultivated their ability to see what's wrong. They can walk past ten presses and hear the one that needs grease. The ability to see subtle deviations may save a machine or even a life. This ability also makes it difficult to see what's right with people's work. One minute praising is

[2] *The One Minute Manager,* by K. Blanchard, Ph.D., and S. Johnson, M.D.

essential for maintenance professionals who want to improve the impact of their leadership. Follow these rules:

tell the person what he/she did right (be very specific),

tell the person how that makes you feel (or the impact of the act), and

do it now.

3. *One Minute Reprimand:* The authors use the word reprimand, which sounds like a serious discipline action which might involve the Union or higher management. This is actually a special type of conversation you would have with a subordinate in order to put them back on course; it does not involve discipline at this point. This is also an opportunity to express your anger and frustration before it can build up and become destructive. The person gets any guilt relieved and knows what is expected. (*Idea:* we are not our behavior.) Before you reprimand, be sure you have the facts. Give the reprimand in a private location.

Be specific, tell the person exactly what behavior made you angry.

Tell them how that behavior made you feel.

Allow a pause—make sure the person understands that the *behavior* was the issue not he/she as a person.

4. Do it now.

Three Thoughts on *The One Minute Manager*

1. *Beware.* Do you believe that you have to be great at it for it to work? The fact is that it will work if you use it. You will improve over time.

2. It will increase productivity because it will tap into people's intelligence and improve motivation. The better your people look, the better you look.

3. Good productivity is a journey, not a destination.

4.

Zero-base Maintenance Budgeting

There is tremendous pressure on maintenance managers to improve their budget performance. Traditional budget methods do not seem to be effective in the maintenance arena because maintenance expenditures are made up of thousands of seemingly unrelated events. Maintenance does not seem to be volume related (higher output equals higher maintenance). The breakdowns and other maintenance activities are hard to predict and do not necessarily reflect what happened last year. To successfully budget (and therefore predict) maintenance expenditures, we must divide the whole maintenance demand into its basic parts.

A zero-base budget breaks the overall demand for maintenance services into its constituents, that is, assets or areas. Look at each asset (or group of like assets) to determine the maintenance exposure. In addition to the unit or asset list, a zero-base budget has allocations for certain areas that are hard to define as individual assets such as the electrical distribution system or the paved parking area and sidewalk.

Prior computerization of maintenance simplifies the construction of a zero-base budget. The computer can easily generate an asset and areas list. Many systems allow you to create classes of equipment where like equipment is aggregated into one line. If the system has been in use for more than a year, you can attach the hours and material dollars for each asset and area. Some systems have a reason for repair (see Chapter 5). The reason for repair would roughly correspond to the categories below. Most systems allow export of the files to a spreadsheet for further manipulation.

All maintenance activity can be traced back to one of the eight demands that follow. Shops that are craft dominated have a more complicated problem. After the budget is completed, they must go back to the individual demands and break out the labor by craft.

The eight reasons for maintenance resources are as follows.

1. *PM—Preventive Maintenance Hours/Materials.* Based on your facility and equipment size, use, construction, and the standard times of the PM activities, you can predict how much time and materials PM's will take. In a TPM shop, some of the PM hours will come from operators. The simplest formula is to multiply the number of services by the time for each service. Also look at the materials used for each service. Include some time for the short repairs that the mechanic will get done during the PM. Since you have some flexibility in scheduling, you can consider PM's as a level demand throughout the year.

    Specifically, PM work includes all the inspection, adjustment, bolt tightening, oiling, cleaning, and readings that are initiated by task lists. The task lists are initiated on a periodic (quarterly, annual) basis.

2. *CM—Corrective Maintenance Hours/Materials.* This is also called scheduled repairs or planned maintenance. As your PM inspectors inspect each part of the facility and all equipment, they write up repairs (deficiencies). These writeups become your backlog of corrective maintenance (CM) for your maintenance schedule. The repairs are considered scheduled repairs as long as they don't interrupt jobs in process.

    You can look at previous years to get an idea of the hours for this activity. Since you have control of the schedule, this demand can be considered level throughout the year. These scheduled repair hours are inserted by equipment, by group of like equipment, or by area.

    There is a tremendous advantage to this type of work because you can plan the work and accumulate several jobs for a location, schedule them together, or assemble several jobs with the same materials or craft (e.g., fix all the small roof problems at several locations) at the same time. I estimate that for every 1 hour spent planning these scheduled jobs, you will save 5 hours on the site.

3. *UM—All Types of User Maintenance (Hours/Materials).* This includes all requests from users/customers from the routine broken pulley on a conveyor to a $1,000,000 catastrophic breakdown. This includes UM-R (*r*outine work) UM-P (small *p*rojects), and UM-B (*b*reakdowns).

UM is the most common source of work in a breakdown-driven organization. Without inspection and inspectors, the users find problems first. Users also are the first to find vandalism, breakdown, and damage. Responsive user complaint handling is essential if you are to be viewed as effective. In fact, most users will judge you entirely on how you respond to their complaints (other benchmarks usually don't have as much impact on their quality of life). UM includes both breakdowns and routine service requests. UM also includes servicing minor user requests for hanging pictures, moving furniture, and other personal service.

At the beginning of the year, budget the same amount of hours of UM as the previous year by asset or category. At the end of the year, you can back off the emergency component of UM as the PM system starts to take effect. For purposes of budgeting, UM creates a level demand. In fact, emergencies will tend to bunch. Many factories use outside contractors to level the demand for UM. In larger facilities, this work will look more and more level. See seasonal demands (SM) for a special case of UM demand.

4. *SM—Seasonal Maintenance Hours/Materials.* This includes all special seasonal demands. Your entire grounds maintenance effort is certainly driven by season. Review of roofing systems before Summer and Winter, or checking air conditioning before Summer, are seasonal demands.

Some businesses are seasonal. Cleaning the candy cane line before it starts up in July would be a seasonal demand. You can also use this category to pick up some percentage of the seasonally driven emergencies or seasonally driven PM. Budget hours at the beginning of each season by asset or group based on history.

5. *RM—Replacement/Remodel Maintenance Hours/Materials.* In some organizations, this category is capital improvement and is handled outside the normal maintenance budget. RM

also includes all maintenance improvements and efficiency improvements. At some point, units which have not been maintained for a period of time or have reached the end of their useful life will have to be rebuilt or replaced. The rebuilding effort should be added to your maintenance budget as a capital replacement line item separate from any current maintenance activity. If workers are doing the modernization to bring units up to PM standards, then the hours will have to be budgeted.

Since you have control of the rebuild schedule, you may be able to use rebuilds as a crew balancing tool. A special case of RM is management decision. This work is generated by a manager when he/she decides to change something in, on, or around a machine, other asset, or the building. The reasons for the decision might range from energy efficiency, improve usage, legal problems, or even a whim (e.g., I hate yellow presses, paint them!).

Maintenance demands are for the whole operation (not tracked by individual, but by location).
After the base demand is cataloged by equipment or area of the plant, look into some of the budget busters below. A well-designed budget can be ruined by excessive social demands generated by visiting dignitaries or a large construction project's effect on the rest of your operation.

6. *SD—Social Demands.* These are sometimes known as "hidden demands" because they don't always show up on work orders; this is also called PS, for Personal Service. Your primary mission is maintenance of the equipment and facility. You may be called upon for other duties in your organization. These duties may include supplying cleanup people, running tours, preparation for visiting dignitaries, providing chauffeur services, picking up or delivering the papers or packages, organizing picnics or work on nonorganization equipment and facilities (charity work). Estimate your hours for these activities.

7. *ED—Expansion Demands.* Any expansion of the size of your facility, size of your workforce, or additions to the scope of your control will add hours to your overall requirements.

New buildings, assembly lines, and major changes to the plant all require startup time. New facilities disrupt current activities as well as take direct time. Adding satellite facilities will result in additional lost time until systems are well in place. Estimate additional time if an expansion is contemplated.

8. *CD—Catastrophic Demands.* It seems that every location has characteristic catastrophes. Add time for one or two catastrophes. You can review your records for the actual amount of time spent in a typical catastrophe. This can include floods, hurricanes, accidents, fires, etc.

How to Set Up a Maintenance Budget

- Start the process by compiling a list of all machinery/equipment that you maintain. As much as possible, arrange the list by department or cost center. This will facilitate report printing at a later stage. If you have a CMMS (Computerized Maintenance Management System), print an asset or equipment list. This list might have hundreds, thousands (or more) entries, depending of the size of your plant.

- Add to this list areas of the plant and site that require maintenance resources that don't lend themselves to the unit concept. Typical areas include roofs, pavement, electrical distribution system, piping, doors/windows, etc.

- Look at the list and see if there are any units that can logically be grouped together. A wire harness assembly plant might have 50 braiding machines of similar usage and vintage. These could logically be aggregated into one line. Putting similar units or areas together simplifies the process and also makes predictions more accurate.

- Collect any maintenance data available by unit or area for the last several years, if available. Your CMMS would facilitate this step. If the data are coming from the CMMS, then see if it has an export capability. Some systems will send data to spreadsheet files without reentry. Inquire if your accounting or cost accounting group can shed any light on the costs to maintain certain areas, departments, assets, or production lines.

- We recommend that this whole mass of information be designed in a computer spreadsheet like Lotus 123, Excel, or Quarto Pro (or equivalent). Create a template to duplicate the form shown in Fig. 3. The equipment, areas, and groups of units/areas are listed in the template. An alternate recommendation would be to enter the data into a database manager. There are advantages to both approaches. Most budgets are usually run from spreadsheets.

- After the individual units and the general assets are listed, add the global lines (that apply to the whole site): social, expansion, catastrophes. Look into your history or estimate the impact of these areas. The three areas can be added as hours and materials, or as percentages, depending on the need. If these areas have traditionally been nonwork order items, now would be a good time to set up the codes to put them on work orders. Once accounted for, these costs can be studied year to year.

- Once assets have been inserted into the template, this document becomes the basis for your zero-based budget. *Backup the filled-in template onto diskette or tape.* You have many hours invested at this point, so make your backups now and keep them up-to-date! The other point is that this computerized list might have other uses, so a copy might be useful for another reason.

- Review each unit, area, or group and estimate your PM, CM, UM, RM, SM cost and hours. A usable history of costs from accounting or from the CMMS greatly simplifies this process.

- Add in your estimates for SD—Social, ED—Expansion, and CD—Catastrophe related demands against the department. These can be as percentages of the above areas or as actual hours and material costs.

- Your material costs are the sum of all material columns, your hours are the sum of all hour columns. You would then apply the costs of your labor, fringe benefits, and maintenance overheads to determine your budget.

ZERO-BASE MAINTENANCE BUDGET   Organization: Department: Name: Page____ of ____

ASSET or GROUP	PM Hours	PM Mat'l	CM Hours	CM Mat'l	UM Hours	UM Mat'l	SM Hours	SM Mat'l	RM Hours	RM Mat'l	TOTAL HOURS	TOTAL MAT'L
Sub-TOTAL												
SOCIAL Costs												
EXPANSION												
CATASTROPHE												
GRAND TOTAL												

Maintech/zerobud frp

Fig. 3.   Zero-base budget form.

When management wants reductions to your budget, you have a new level of discussion. All changes need to be justified in terms of higher or lower levels of service on individual assets or areas. Now when cuts are needed, you can talk about which assets will be allowed to deteriorate or which departments will not be served as well. Almost every business has deferred maintenance. You may see a problem slowly developing and put off the work. You could be short of funds, be planning a major rehabilitation, planning to sell the unit or property, or lack the requisite skills. Some organizations run their whole operation with excessive amounts of deferred maintenance. Distribute your zero-base budget to the users, staff, and top management for comments.

If your current actual hours available comprise only a small percentage of your budgeted demand, then something will have to be done. Either deterioration is taking place or your customers are unsatisfied (or both). One solution is to use contractors to make up the shortfall. Some organizations are using this strategy to maintain maximum flexibility.

Using the Budget to Schedule the Need for Outsourcing

Some organizations use outsourcing strategies whereby they crew for 75%–80% of demand and use outside vendors during peak periods. The most effective way to predict the need for contract labor is to recast the budget on a monthly basis. Using the hours per month, you can see which months will exceed your crew's available hours.

The process is similar to a staffing exercise. If your core crew has 1400 hours available per month, the contractor would have to supply and labor above 1400 hours. The budget will show which months it would be likely that contracting will be needed. Delaying project work can be used to minimize contractor needs in a given month.

5.

Maintenance Information Flow

Where does your work come from? Several sources are internal (PM tasks and corrective maintenance) and the rest are external to the maintenance department. A study of your information flow might show where requests for work could fall through the cracks. It would also show where you are not capturing the minimum amount of information to efficiently dispatch maintenance workers. (See Fig. 4.)

All requests for service should converge in the maintenance control center and be reviewed by a single person or group. If you use a team structure, then the team point person on planning and scheduling should review the requests. Emergencies should be handled as directly as possible. The goal of the system is to serve the customer efficiently, with minimum overhead.

Maintenance information flow is important, regardless of the size of the factory. Large organizations might have whole departments providing each function. Small ones can literally use four clipboards for all maintenance activity. (See Fig. 5.) All information is routed as follows.

1. Incoming work requests are taken from the "In-Bin" and are reviewed for authorization, parts ordering, planning. Time/date stamping should take place when a job is placed into the in-bin. The in-bin should be scanned frequently for high-priority work that no one mentioned. The in-bin is the funnel into the rest of the system.

   One function of this step is planning. Planning might be as easy as making sure that the materials are in stock on a

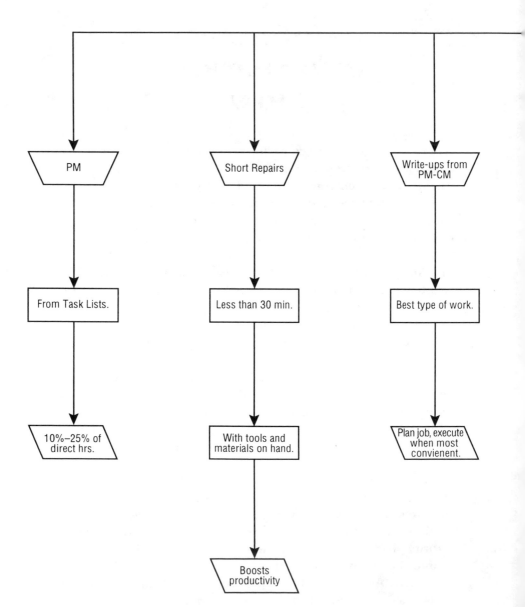

Fig. 4.   Sources of maintenance work.

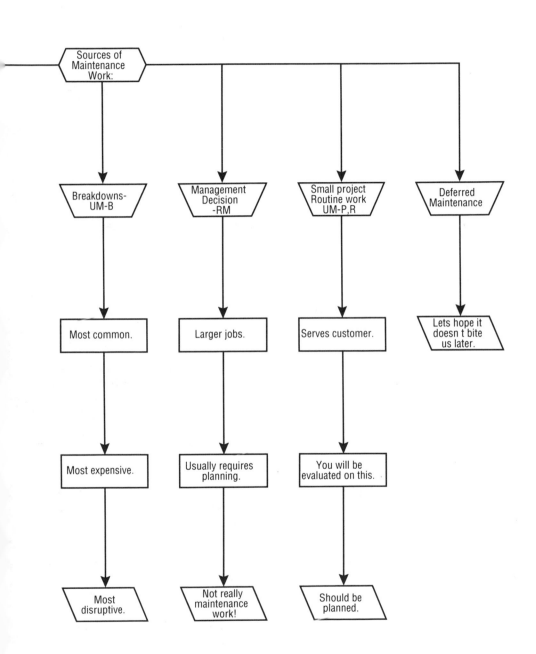

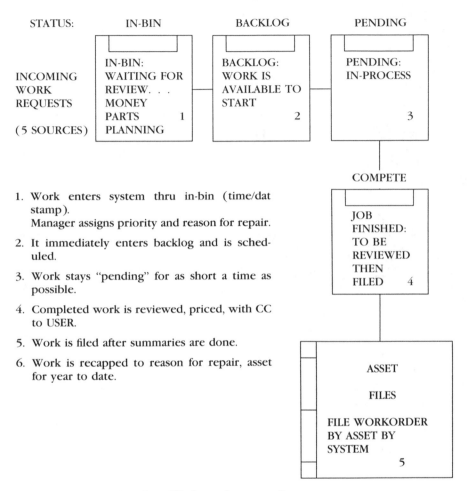

Fig. 5.   Clipboard control system.

machine repair, or as complex as coordination of contractors and employees on a model change in an auto plant. Once the work order is past this function, it will be scheduled for action. Work orders that you have not decided when to do should stay in the in-bin. Some organizations keep files of wish-list jobs in case some resources are freed up.

Some computer systems maintain status codes for each job. These status codes follow the job through all of the steps before the job is released to the shop. Status codes could include: Waiting to be Planned, Waiting for Engineering, Waiting for P.O. to be Issued, Waiting for Material to be Received, Waiting for Weekend (or Night or Summer), Waiting Until Shutdown, Ready for Fill-In Assignment.[1]

2. The "Backlog" clipboard is all work available to start. All backlog jobs have been authorized, parts are available, priority has been set, and planning (if required) has been done. Once the job is issued to the contractor or staff mechanic, it then moves to the "pending" clipboard. Managing the backlog is an important way to manage an entire maintenance department. It is essential that the available backlog not fall below a few days nor increase to greater than two weeks per tradesperson. Too low a backlog will encourage the tradespeople to stretch out the work that is left to avoid layoff. Too high a backlog will cause the customers to suffer unreasonable delays for routine work requests.

3. Jobs in the "Pending" clipboard have been issued to employees or to contractors, and should be completed in a short time. This clipboard should be reviewed regularly for stuck jobs. A stuck job that stays stuck is a problem for the manager and the user. Extra effort (sometimes an outside contractor is needed) may be used to unstick these jobs.

4. The jobs, once completed, are costed and posted to the various recap sheets for the Asset File System. All sketches, photographs, and booklets (that come with thermocouple, PLC modules, pumps, etc.) go in the file. Costing and root failure analysis notes also go into the file in the appropriate section.

Typical Benchmarks

- Respond to 99% of emergency service calls within X hours. Carry it to pending state. Secure building, machine, and user.

- Respond to 99% of routine service calls within X days. Carry it to pending state. Secure machine, building, and user.

- Clear "Pending" clipboard weekly.

[1] Ideas for additional status codes are from Don Nyman in his seminar text, *Maintenance Management.*

Maintenance Work Order

The primary purpose of a work order is communication with the mechanic. Work orders give the mechanic written instructions which include location, description of the problem, who to see, authorization to proceed, and a contact phone number.

You need a work order or write-up sheet because the write-up is the basis of all future analysis. Every hour worked by an employee or a contractor should be accounted for on one of the four types of documents. Work orders are your unique history; having them easily available for research or review pays dividends in root cause analysis and continuous improvement programs. The work order can also be a tremendous benefit in the following areas.

1. *Cost Collection.* All of the labor and parts are recorded on the work order. Charging all time and materials is a more accurate view of a process's real profitability. Cost is allocated by asset number, department, or by plant. The work order can be used as the basis of a charge-back system. Charge-back is an excellent way to highlight departments that use an inordinate amount of maintenance resources.

2. *Proof of Safety and Proof of Compliance with Codes and Statutes.* When there is an accident or some other catastrophe, officials will want to see your maintenance records. While having records will not remove the pain of a catastrophe, being able to prove that you did what you could will make you feel somewhat better. It will show the authorities and your management that you were doing your job. Properly executed PM records can significantly reduce your share of the liability if you are involved in litigation. The truth is: a plant with a well-documented maintenance effort will be safer and is more likely to be in compliance with codes and statues.

3. *Job, Project, and Mechanic Management, Scheduling, and Control Document.* The work orders show the progress of a larger job and facilitate control. On a larger job you can write all the subtasks on write-up forms and use the forms to manage the job. Companies will visually recreate the

PERT or CPM chart with the work orders to help manage the shutdown or major repair.

4. *Letting the User Know What is Happening on Their Job.* Work orders aid communication with the user. Sending a copy of the document after it enters backlog shows the user that you are working on their problem, as well as improves user relations. We recommend that you send another copy to the user when the job is complete. Follow the example of a major pharmaceutical company and put a quality/satisifaction survey on the back of the user's copy of the completed work order. When the work order is folded, the survey is on the outside. Questions include: were you satisfied? was the job done in a professional manner? was the mechanic on time with any appointment? any suggestions?

5. *Provides History for Various Assets and Their Components.* The history derived from the work orders tells you which types of compressors last longer, which valves are easier to rebuild, and many other useful bits of information. It only takes a few years before you have enough history to make decisions. History can be used to compare different conditions (such as differrent PM intervals or different lubrications).

6. *The Work Orders Might Jog Your Institutional Memory.* The work order history also is useful when you have not done a repair for an extended period, and the work order from an earlier repair is available. It could be helpful for locating vendors, planning, and research into techniques.

7. *Authorization for Parts and Special Tools.* If you use contractors, this allows them to buy materials against your account and to secure special tools. In large organizations, the work order is authorization to the store room to release the part. It could also be the initiator of a material requisition if the item is not in stock.

8. *Can Become a Training Document for Less Skilled Workers.* By reviewing what was done for each type of complaint, the mechanics can see what kind of problems they will have

to fix and what parts were used. Summaries of actual work orders can be used to design a training course by pinpointing the most likely repairs for training. If the work is formally planned, then the work order will have job steps that might also be useful for training.

9. *Provides Data for Root Failure Analysis.* When a recurrent problem plagues you, the work orders will show you how often, how expensive, what parts were used, and how long the repair took. This information helps (in several ways) track down the root cause and identify the financial exposure. Without a work order, you have to rely on the memory and conversations of the mechanics (who might be on several shifts).

10. *Insurance Recovery.* If you have a fire or other claim, the insurance company can use the write-up to determine the amount to pay you. If you claim that an insurable event caused disruption to maintenance activity, then an analysis of the work orders might provide the proof needed by the insurance company.

11. *Warranty Recovery.* Many items that you buy have warranties. The work order can sometimes be used to document the problem for warranty recovery. In some cases, a large number of premature failures could initiate warranty recovery for all items in that batch. Some warranties include labor, and some just include materials.

12. *Feedback to Planners.* The work order tells the planner what actually happened and how long it took. This feedback can improve the effectiveness of the planning function. For this reason, many facilities that have planners close out work orders and enter the data into the computer.

13. *Source Document to Reconstruct what Really Happened.* We want to get to the bottom of every expensive or disruptive failure. A properly filled out work order will facilitate this analysis.

14. *Source of Data About Hidden Demands.* The maintenance department is frequently recruited into playing roles such as

driver, pick-up person, furniture mover, personal servant, boat polisher, picnic set-up/clean-up crew, security crew, and so on. These are special jobs that need to be tracked. For a Southern manufacturer, significant money was saved by hiring a limousine company to pick up visitors at the airport rather than use the mechanic. The savings were in time lost, parking fees, disruption to ongoing jobs, auto costs, and insurance; and most of the passengers preferred being picked up by professionals.

15. *Evidence in Court.* The maintenance information system provides data for court hearings on liability claims, injury claims, breach of contract claims, etc.

Design of Work Orders

If you design your own document, be sure to do the following.

- Use wide lines so that the mechanic can fill in information easily.

- Size the document to fit on a clipboard if you expect the mechanic to write on it (or buy special clipboards).

- Place your organization's name on top to be more professional.

- Use check-off boxes where possible to reduce writing and to improve completeness.

- Consider using bar codes to speed data entry. Bar codes also increase accuracy.

- Consider the paperless work order systems, where everything is typed or scanned into terminals around the shop (or use handheld terminals that are radio linked to the network).

- For large facilities without networked computerized work order systems, designate and use fax machines to transmit work orders around the facility. Never forget that the prime reason for work orders is to provide written communication with the tradesperson. The message would be "Jack, please go to fax #391 for your next job." In a computerized network, mechanics would walk to a terminal and punch up the work order themselves.

Four Types of Work Order Forms Serve Different Purposes

Maintenance Write-Up Form (MWU)

This form would be filled out by the PM inspector or surveyor during the inspection. It could also be filled out by a maintenance office worker for a called-in complaint. This is the most common type of work order. During an emergency, the documentation would be completed when the job is completed. Maintenance departments need to conduct periodic classes in correctly filling out this document. The better this is filled out, the easier and more accurate will be any subsequent analysis.

The Maintenance Log Sheet (MLS)

This form could be carried by the craftsperson for all the short repairs done in the course of a day. TPM attempts to record intermittent work stoppages. These stoppages are usually corrected by short, unrecorded adjustments and repairs. This is the method to document these small problems. It could also be carried by regular vendors to record all of the little things that they complete. Also, major problems are sometimes covered up by numerous short repairs or adjustments. These little things add up to significant dollars on an annual basis. Not completing short repairs is also the main reason for user dissatisfaction and subsequent maintenance manager hassles.

The Standing Work Order (SWO)

This form can be used for jobs that are done routinely with known labor and materials. Examples would be a machine startup every Monday morning, or a walkthrough done every week to look at the grounds and pick up litter. A single "standing work order" might be good for a week, month, or longer. These are usually routine jobs that aid the user.

The String PM Work Order (SPMWO)

String PM's are the only work orders that are not unit based. The string is a group of like assets that are strung together for PM purposes. A vibration route or filter change route are examples. The string PM is one of the hardest to account for in computerized maintenance systems. Usually the CMMS allows the input of only one asset number.

Note: The PM task list could be a form of standing work order or a string PM work order. The time and materials necessary should be captured on a special PM work order form.

Examples of the types of work order are shown in Figs. 6–9.

Explanation of All Fields on the Work Order forms

To review, there are four types of work order forms:

- Maintenance Write-Up (MWU)

- Maintenance Log Sheet (MLS) for Short Jobs

- Standing Work Order (SWO)

- String PM Work Order (SPMWO)

All work order forms are divided into three sections. *Header:* Information known before the repair starts. *Body:* Feedback from mechanic. *Summary:* Information added up in dollars, hours, or both.

Header of Work Order (Information is Usually Known Before the Repair Begins)

Asset Number

All assets in the plant have unique identifiers called asset numbers. Since the number is unique, it is the best way to describe the machine needing attention.

#MWU	LOCATION:		DATE:		TIME DOWN:
MAINTENANCE WRITE-UP			DOWNTIME? Y N		TIME BACK IN SERVICE

P R I O R T Y	USER:			PHONE:			DOWN HOURS:	

	100 DGR FIRE SFTY	80 STOP PROD	70 SAFETY OR CODE VIOLAT.	60 PM	50 EFFIC IMPROV.	40 COMFOR	30 COSMETIC		OTHER PRIO	**SPECIAL** LOCK-OUT
					DAMAG		CHG USE			PERMIT REQUIRED

REASON FOR WRITE-UP	SCHEDULED WORK									UNSCHEDULED								CONFINED SPACE
	PM	CM	UM-P	R	RM-M	I	E	U	OTHR	CL	GN	UM	PS	DR	DU	MU	OB	OTHER

SYSTEM:	REQUESTED BY:
	DATE REQUIRED:
	CHARGE-BACK ACCOUNT:

DESCRIPTION OF WORK REQUESTED:

SKILL LEVEL	UNSKILLED	MAINTENANCE PERSON	LICENSED TRADES	ENGINEER OR OTHER	CONTRACTOR:

TIME IN	TIME OUT	HRS	DESCRIPTION OF WORK	TOTAL PRICE	PARTS & MATERIALS: DESCRIPTION/PART NO.	QUAN
TOTALS			* CHGRT( ) = +		= TOTAL THIS W/O $	

WHAT WAS FOUND: NOTES FROM MECHANIC

DATE COMPLETED:	INSPECTED BY:

Fig. 6. Maintenance work order.

MAINTENANCE LOG SHEET FOR SHORT JOBS

DATE	TO

MLS#

NAME:

LINE DATE	ASSET	LOCATION/ SYSTEM	USER NAME	WORK REQUESTED WORK COMPLETED	REAS/ PRITY	MATERIALS	IN OUT TOTAL
1							
2							
3							
4							
5							
6							
7							
8							
9							
10							

maximum job time 30 minutes, prepare write-up over 30 minutes

Fig. 7. Maintenance log sheet.

Location

The location of the work should be included on all work requests. In some cases, this is the location of the asset; in other cases, it is the location *on* the asset (for a large asset). This eliminates the problem of the mechanic going to the wrong area to do a repair. Location means where the unit is that requires work. An address or building number should be included as required.

#SWO	STANDING WORK ORDER					DATE OPENED		DATE CLOSED
	USER: PHONE:					LOCATION:		SPECIAL LOCK-OUT
PRIORITY:	70 SAFETY OR CODE VIOLATION	60 PM DAMAG	50 EFFIC. IMPROV	40 COMFOR				PERMIT REQUIRED CONFINED SPACE
REASON FOR WRITE-UP	PM CM RM UMR CL GN OTHER					DOWNTIME REQUIRED: Y N		OTHER
SYSTEM:				CHARGE-BACK ACCOUNT?:			REQUESTED BY:	

DESCRIPTION OF WORK REQUESTED:

SKILL LEVEL	UNSKILLED	MAINTENANCE PERSON	LICENSED TRADES	ENGINEER OR OTHER	CONTRACTOR:

LABOR ESTIMATE: MATERIAL REQUIREMENTS:

ESTIMATED BY:

DATE	INIT	TIME	DOWN TIME	MATERIAL	DATE	INIT	TIME	DOWN TIME	MATERIAL
TOTAL DOWN TIME					TOTAL DOWNTIME				
TOTAL (HRS1		+HRS2		) *CHGRT	+(MAT'L		MAT'L		=

ATTACH PAYMENT HISTORY FOR CONTRACTOR

Fig. 8. Standing work order.

#SFW	BUILDING, LOCATION OR ASSET			WHEN DONE CHECK OFF	DOWN TIME	COMMENTS
STRING PM						
WORK ORDER	1.					
	2.					
DATE	3.					
	4.					
COMMENTS:	5.					
	6.					
	7.					
	8.					
	9.					
	10.					

PRIORITY:		70 SAFETY OR CODE VIOLATION	60 PM DAMAGE	50 EFFIC. OR IMPROV	OTHER	DOWNTIME REQUIR Y N HOURS:	SPECIAL REQUIR LOCKOUT
REASON FOR WRITE-UP:	PM	UMR	CL	GN	OTHER	DATE REQUESTED:	PERMIT CONFINED ENTRY
CHARGE BACK TO ACCOUNT			REQUESTED BY:				OTHER
		SKILL LEVEL	UNSKILLED	MAINTENANCE PERSON	LICENSED TRADES	ENGINEER OR OTHER	

DESCRIPTION OF STRING:

TASK:	MATERIALS:
HOURS: CHARGE RATE:$	MATERIALS $:

TOTAL THIS W/O: $

Fig. 9.   String PM work order.

Date, Date Opened, Date Closed

The date should be when the dispatcher wrote up the form or entered the request. For user write-ups, the date should be when the request was received by maintenance department. Many systems time/date stamp all incoming work requests. This is an excellent idea since one useful benchmark is the average response time for each priority work. On standing orders, the date opened is when the work order was initiated, and the date closed is when the work order is full. Usually a new one is opened at that time. A standing order might stay open a whole week, month, or longer, depending on how the information is used.

Downtime

Do we want to track downtime on this asset. If checked "Y" (yes), then keep "Time Down" and "Time Back in Service." If checked "N" (no), then ignore those blocks.

Time Down, Time Back in Service

Where downtime is important, the time down is recorded. In these situations, the request should be time stamped when it is received by maintenance. Production might spend an hour trying to get the equipment back in service before calling maintenance. The difference might be a significant source of conflict. Time back in service should be when the unit is completed and available for production. The actual definition of these times is an item of discussion between production control, production, and maintenance.

User, Phone

Unnecessary hours are spent each year trying to get access to equipment, units, and locked rooms. In other cases, the mechanic needs to talk to the operator or production supervisor to clarify the requested service. All work requested needs a contact person to be included in the package.

System

This describes in more detail what will be worked on, if known. Information on system codes can be gotten from the asset detail sheet, where they are called subcomponents. The system code helps the maintenance analyst look for root causes. This would usually not be used on the log sheet. Examples of "Systems" would be circulating pump on a boiler, hydraulic pump on an injection molder, or lubrication injection system on a mechanical punch press. If work orders are generated in the maintenance control center, the person writing the request would also include manufacturer, model, and serial number (if that information is available and relevant).

Priority

Priority helps assign work where there is more work than people. It ensures that vital work is not overlooked in the rush of urgent (but unimportant) jobs. Priority systems have a habit of being abused so that users can get their work done faster (if they write up their own work orders). Typical priority codes are as follows.

100: Fire, safety, health (clear and present danger with automatic overtime authorized until the hazard is removed).

80: Breakdowns that stop production, overtime authorized.

70: Fire/safety/health (potential danger to user, public, employees, or environment); statute or code violation, OSHA violation, EPA.

60: PM activity; potential breakdown including core damage, or loss (all types of minor leaks, decay that will get worse).

50: Efficiency improvement, machinery improvements, project work, reengineering.

40: Comfort, change use.

30: Cosmetics.

In some systems, the criticality of the equipment affects the priority.

Reason for Write-Up (or Repair Reason)

All work orders are initiated for a reason. These reasons should be noted on each work order. The reason is captured for future analysis. Remember that when you pay a mechanic or a contractor, you buy your maintenance history. Repair reason allows you to analyze your demand for work and, hopefully, make those adjustments that will save you money! Possible reasons to initiate a work order (you can specify your own codes for unique repair reasons) include the following.

Code   Description

SCHEDULED ACTIVITY (activity that was known about at least 1 day in advance and can be planned):

PM   1. PM (preventive maintenance) task list activity such as inspection, lube, adjustment, and survey (an initial PM inspection).

CM   2. Corrective maintenance (includes scheduled maintenance known 1–2 days in advance, when PM worker finds a potential or impending problem).

UM-R   3. User maintenance—Routine work or standing work order (known work done every week).
UM-P   User maintenance—Project work requested by production (usually small jobs, can be planned). Larger projects are considered RM-type maintenance.

RM   4. Rehabilitation maintenance, rebuild, capital project from management decision.
RM-M   Modernize equipment to shop spec.
RM-I   Installation of new equipment.
RM-E   Efficiency improvement.
RM-U   User initiated modification.

CL   5. Cleaning machines and shop, sweeping up, etc.

GN   6. Grounds, including cleaning, mowing, exterior, snow removal, etc.

NONSCHEDULED ACTIVITY

UM-B   7. User maintenance—Breakdown (requiring immediate action). UM-B could be jam-up, slow down, leak, quality problem, immediate safety danger, etc.

PS   8. Personal service, errands, minor jobs around office.

D-R   9. Reported damage (someone made a mistake and broke something and reported it).

D-U   10. Unreported damage, no report, includes vandalism, sabotage.

MU   11. Misapplied use, wrong component for job.

OB   12. Other breakdown, including code violation, safety audit, OSHA inspection, PM inspector finds imminent danger or breakdown (cannot be scheduled).

Example

In a recent review of repair reasons in a fabrication shop, we found the following hours.

Reason for Repair	1993	1994	1995
1. PM Activity	0	560	940
2. PM—Survey*	0	40	40
3. CM—Corrective Maintenance	0	2978	2695
4. UM-R** Routine Work or Standing Work Order	4706	4245	1675
5. UM-P Small User Projects	1200	1225	1675
5. RM— Management Decision	1323	4580	1521
6. Vandalism/ Damage	690	345	267
A. D-R Reported Damage	120	240	290
B. D-U Unreported Damage	810	585	527
9. UM-B Customer/ User Complaint	5970	2250	1556
10. OB—OSHA Inspection	611	240	58
Totals	14,620 hrs	16,703 hrs	11,687 hrs

Explore the several trends in these labor statistics: which trends are you convinced are real, and which could turn around in a "bad" year?

*Survey is a complete walkthrough of a facility to see the "big" maintenance picture.

**Routine work has a known duration, such as 2 hour startup, shift assigned as an area mechanic. It can also have a known work requirement like mopping a hallway, changing a die. There is usually only a limited amount of maintenance work per se involved.

Description of
Work Requested

It is important to train your requesters to report the observed condition with as much supporting detail as possible. People tend to blame machines, systems, and components if these things have failed in the past. They also tend to blame the part of the system that they are least comfortable with. This can mislead the mechanic. Instruct the requesters to note what was happening just before the breakdown.

Example: A process control company whose systems controlled oil terminals received a call (in the middle of the night, of course) that the main computer shut off and the blending subsystem was off line. The mechanic arrived at the terminal and spent several hours doing a complete system analysis. Everything seemed fine except that the output was not turning on the pump on one of the products being blended. The mechanic also noticed that the gauging system seemed out of range. The second product's pump was not activating because the source tank for the first product was empty! The system was acting exactly as designed. The report of a broken main computer misled the mechanic for several hours. For good descriptions of work, report to the maintenance department only the observed rather than the inferred information.

If you design your own work order, be sure there are separate fields for work requested and work performed. This will ensure the integrity of the database by keeping the customer's perception level out of the history file as a cause or effect. We want to collect the work requested for another reason. At some point, we will be able to build a table between the job requested and the job performed. We can then give the mechanic the highest probability problem based on what was requested (regardless of whether or not the requested work is "right").

Idea for Action: If someone calls in with a problem, have a list of questions to try to filter out the nonmaintenance and frivolous calls. Be sure that a copy of the questions is reviewed during the customer/user orientation. This could cut the number of actual service calls. Include "not plugged in" problems, procedures for overloads, material outage, wrong tooling/materials.

Requested By

The work requester needs to be authorized and preferably trained in the maintenance request system. Depending on your organization, the requester will be you, your user, or staff. Remember, the better the request, the less likely a wild goose chase will follow.

Date Wanted

When is the job requested? Restrict unreasonable due dates (such as ASAP), and authorize overtime and, if necessary, a contractor.

Charge-Back to Account

The accounting system might require different types of repairs be coded or charged to different accounts. Also, many service requests are paid for by the user's budget. These charge-backs need to be well documented since some of the charge-backs will be questioned.

Skill Level

Certain jobs require higher skill levels or special licenses. The manager/planner should evaluate the skill needed. Some localities require licensed trade for certain jobs. If a contractor is used, the work order would be attached to the purchase order. The same information is required for in-house or contracted jobs.

Labor Estimate, Material/Tool Requirements (On Standing Work Order)

This block should include a description of the work to be done, broken into logical steps. Each step is estimated. The labor estimate is determined by experience, observation, or study. The tool requirements alert the technician to what tools are likely to be needed. This block should include a description of the estimated materials used and their costs. Small supplies would be included. All major or recurring parts should be included. Materials for standing jobs should be known in detail, with accuracy from observation or engineering study.

Body of Work Order (Information Known Only After the Repair is Complete)

Time In, Time Out, Hours

The mechanic should write the time he/she arrives and leaves, and the hours to do the job. If a mechanic leaves a job to get parts, he/she should clock out and start a new line—getting parts; the mechanic clocks in upon return to the job site to complete the work.

Date, Initials, Time, Downtime, Material

On the standing order, the job will be done several times on different days and logged to the same document. Each time the job is done, the date, initials of the mechanic, the elapsed time of the job itself, total elapsed time the unit is down (when "Downtime Required" block is checked), and the material used is logged to the open order.

Description of Work, Description of String

Give a quick description of the work to be done. A typical job might be described as: 1) look into problem, 2) get parts, 3) install parts. Use the same standard for expressing time (use hours/minutes or hours/tenth). In the string PM work order, include a quick description of the string, like "vibration route in the press department."

Task, Materials

On a string PM work order, each task is written out with the materials needed. Attach extra sheets for longer strings. Keep in mind that string PM is usually a few simple tasks on several machines.

Quantity Parts and Materials, Price

Whenever parts or materials are used, they are recorded on the work order in these columns. Include the total price for all parts used. When an item is drawn from stock, then you have to look up the price and insert it. Put in the part number where replacement parts are used, and where you think you might need to use the number again.

What was Found: Notes from Mechanic, Comments

Frequently, the mechanic fixes something or finds something not anticipated by the work requester (a broken pump call results in replacement of a power supply on a PLC rack). This allows the mechanic to give feedback as to what was really found to be part of the permanent record for the asset. These notes are essential for root failure analysis.

Date Completed, Inspector

The job has to be closed out by an inspection. The inspector can be the mechanic, an inspector, a satisfied user, or the supervisor. In a major oil refinery, the PM crew signed off on all repairs before the unit could be returned to service. The thought was that safety was a big issue, and the PM crew was trained in safe return of equipment to service. In this refinery, they were also an elite group in terms of years of service, skills, dedication, and pay.

Summary of Work Order
(Calculations After Job is Turned In)

Totals

Add up all the hours and note in the totals. If you use a contractor, put in their charge-out rate (if known, otherwise put in the total dollars). Extend the material total and add that to the labor total for a work order total.

CHGRT

The charge rate is the burdened labor rate for your facility. In some cases, each level mechanic or trade has its own charge rate. The charge rate should include labor, fringes, overhead, and a factor for the ratio of payroll hours to work order hours. Charge rate is also the amount that the contractor charges you per hour. If you have just one charge for the whole job, skip this part and fill in *Total this W/O.*

TOTALS (from the Standing Work Order)

This row allows you to calculate the total cost of the work order. The formula adds the hours from the two columns together and multiply times the CHGRT (charge-out rate) for total labor cost. There is room to total both material columns for a total material cost. The grand sum is the cost of the work order.

Recap Sheets (Usually Kept on the Computer, and Run When Needed)

If you are rigorous about filling out your work orders (of all types), you will start to build a written history that can provide significant benefit. The benefit is in improved decision making. It is easier to make decisions with real hard data (as opposed to the last anecdote you remember), and it is very difficult to make good decisions without hard data.

Computerized Maintenance Information Systems should provide both types of Recap reports. Most systems allow many different types of analysis reports available in many formats. Figs. 10 and 11 show examples of two common recap sheets that provide valuable information.

Recap of Jobs (By Machine or Asset, Floor or Area)

This sheet is developed from the four types of work orders. Summaries of each work order or log are recapped to the appropriate asset's sheet. Since this looks at the number of incidents, all log entries done at the same time can be summarized. Log entries that

RECAP OF JOBS

ASSET NAME:					ASSET NUMBER:				
ASSET DESCRIPTION:					DATE FROM:		TO:		
LINE DATE	MECHAN NAME	WO#/ SYSTEM	REQUEST NAME	WORK REQUESTED WORK COMPLETED	RSN PTY	HOURS	MAT'L $	TOTAL $	
1									
2									
3									
4									
5									
6									
7									
8									
9									
10									

W/O# - WORK ORDER NUMBER (MWO1234, SWO234, ML1291, ETC.)
RSN - REASON FOR REPAIR FROM W/O (PM,CM,UM, ETC)
PTY - PRIORITY FROM W/O (1 TO 9)
HOURS- TOTAL HOURS FOR W/O
MAT'L- COST OF ALL MATERIALS (EXAMPLE $12.00)
TOTAL- COST OF W/O (EXAMPLE $45.78)

CC:
ASSET FILE
IN LOG BOOK ON MACHINE

Fig. 10. Recap of jobs.

	ASSET	DATE	REFERENCE	PM	CM	UMR	RMM	RMI	RME	CL	GN	UM	PS	DR	DU	MU	OB
REASON FOR REPAIR **RECAP**	DATE FROM		TO														
1																	
2																	
3																	
4																	
5																	
6																	
7																	
8																	
9																	
10																	
11																	
12																	
13																	
14																	
15																	
16																	
17																	
18																	
19																	
20																	
21																	
		TOTALS															
				PM	CM	UMR	RMM	RMI	RME	CL	GN	UM	PS	DR	DU	MU	OB

PM-PREVENTIVE MAINTENANCE
CM-CORRECTIVE MAINTENANCE
UMR- USER MAIN ROUTINE   UM-USER MAINTENANCE   MU-MIS-APPLIED USE
RMM-REHAB   PS-PERSONAL SERVICE   CL-CLEANING
RMI-GOOD IDEA   DR-REPORTED DAMAGE   GN-GROUNDS
RME-EFFICIENCY   DU-UNREPORTED DAMAGE   OB-OTHER BREAKDOWN

Fig. 11. Repair reason recap.

take place on a separate trip should be entered on a separate line of the recap sheet.

The repeat job is the nemesis of the maintenance department. These jobs need to be reviewed as a group to detect trends, mechanic incompetence, underlying mechanical problems, or user problems. Many times you will see that jobs are related to each other (such as overloads and seemingly unrelated wiring problems in other parts of the facility).

Reason for Repair Recap (Complete for Each Type of Asset, for Example, All 10 HP Water Pumps, the Automated Warehouse, etc.)

The "Reason for Repair Recap" is filled out for every work order. The fields "Address," "Date," "Ref" (the work order number) are transferred from the work order. Locate the reason for the repair and enter the total dollars for the work order. The "Comment" field can include short comments or references to attached notes.

Each work order was initiated for a reason. Investigation of the reasons uncovers the sources of your work, and may recommend solutions that would reduce your work load.

Repair History Jacket

The information in the asset jacket, book, or folder can be kept on the computer. Some organizations also keep the folder in paper form because of all the little sketches and as-built doodles. The physical location is less important than the ease with which you can get to the data. The file should include the following.

1. Survey sheet.

2. Equipment record card or contents of the equipment master file from the CMMS.

3. Printouts of all work orders (actual working copies with notes if possible).

4. Copy of all engineering data relating to unit.

5. Wiring diagrams, as-built drawings, documented modifications.

6. Planned work, shut-down work lists, past shut-down lists.

7. PM list.

8. Planning guides for various repairs, and feedback on results of repairs.

9. A wish list of things you would like to change about the asset.

10. PM justification (why the unit should be on PM).

11. Justification for each item on the PM list based on history, experience, and economics.

12. Copy of recap sheets for that asset.

13. Possibly several physical files.

The files should be located in the Maintenance Technical Library. The *Maintenance Technical Library (MTL)* is a place where maintenance technicians can have access to repair history jackets, equipment manuals, parts lists, assembly drawings. The MTL should have large reference tables, shelving for books and catalogs, and legal-sized file cabinets. In addition, the MTL should be the location of a copy of plant drawings, site drawings, vendor catalogs, handbooks, engineering textbooks, etc. If you have computerized maintenance, stores, or purchasing, CADD, CAM, then a terminal (after access is negotiated) could be located in the MTL.

Considerations for the MTL [2]:

• Protect it from fire, flood, theft (consider fireproof file cabinets).

• Use some kind of sign-out system if material must be removed.

• Make it someone's responsibility to keep it up-to-date.

[2] *Maintenance Management,* by Jay Butler, published by University Seminar Center (address in Resource section).

- Manage the revisions so that all copies are updated (coordinate with ISO 9000).

When the MTL is set up, you will have: a ready reference for make-versus-buy decisions; repair history; repair parts reference with history; repair methods referral; planning information source; time standard development; data bank for continuous improvement efforts; maintenance improvement team headquarters.

6.
Managing PM (Preventive Maintenance)

Understanding Preventive Maintenance

What *is* PM? PM is a series of tasks that either extend the life of an asset (for example, greasing a gearbox) or detect that an asset has had critical wear and is going to fail or break down (for example, a quarterly inspection shows a small leak from a pump seal, which allows you to repair it before a catastrophic breakdown).

Common tasks associated with PM are as follows.

Type of Task	Example
Inspection	Look for leaks in hydraulic system
Predictive maintenance	Scan all electrical connections with infrared
Cleaning	Remove debris from machine
Tightening	Tighten anchor bolts
Operate	Advance heat control on injection molding machine until heater activates
Adjustment	Adjust tension on drive belt
Take readings	Record readings on amperage
Lubrication	Add 2 drops of oil to stitcher
Scheduled replacement	Remove and replace pump every 5 years
Interview operator	Ask operator how machine is operating
Analysis	Perform history analysis of a type of machine

These tasks are assembled into task lists. Each task is marked off when it is completed. There should always be room on the bottom or side of the task list to note comments. Actionable items should be highlighted.

These tasks should be directed at how the asset will fail. The rule is that the tasks should repair the unit's most expensive, most likely, or most dangerous failure modes. (*Caveat:* There will still be failures and breakdowns even with the best PM systems. Your goal is to reduce the breakdowns to minimal levels, and convert the breakdowns that are left into learning experiences to improve your delivery of maintenance service.)

PM systems also include the following.

1. Maintaining a record-keeping system to track PM, failures, and equipment utilization. Creating baselines for other analysis activity.

2. All types of predictive activities. These include inspection, taking measurements, and inspecting parts for quality; and analysis of the oil, temperature, and vibration. Recording all data from predictive activity for trend analysis.

3. Short or minor repairs up to 30 minutes in length. This is a great boost to productivity since there is no additional travel time.

4. Writing up any conditions that require attention (conditions which will lead, or potentially lead, to a failure). Write-ups of machine condition.

5. Scheduling and actually doing repairs written up by PM inspectors.

6. Using the frequency and severity of failures to refine the PM task list.

7. Continual training and upgrading of inspector's skills, as well as improvements to PM technology.

One point that is commonly missed is that PM is a way station to the ultimate goal of maintainability improvement. PM can be an expensive option because it requires constant inputs of labor, mate-

rials, and downtime. The ultimate goal of maintenance is high reliability without the inputs. Understand what PM is trying to accomplish, and know the critical wear point.

PM systems are designed for two purposes: to detect the location of the critical wear point along the wear curve and, by proper
lubrication, cleaning, tightening, and adjustment, to defer critical
wear. Critical wear will sometimes manifest itself as an inability to
hold a measurement or tolerance.

If we could look into a machine or electrical system and know
exactly how and where it is wearing (wearing means failing), then
we wouldn't have to keep inspecting it. We would just lubricate,
clean, tighten, and adjust it; then, at the right instant, we'd replace
the part just before it fails. Note that a large machine has many critical wear points for each component (see Fig. 12).

Examples of Critical Wear

Engines: When motor oil has enough metal particles to hone the
inside of the engine, failure is close behind. You push off the critical
wear point by changing the filter.

Belts: As soon as slippage starts, failure is accelerated. You adjust
the belt to push off the critical wear point.

Bearings: Once wear deforms the ball in the bearing, it will get
worse and destroy the entire bearing relatively quickly. You replace

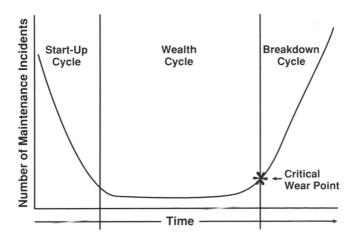

Fig. 12.   Critical wear point chart.

it to push off the critical wear point on the rest of the system (such as a fan failure after the bearing goes).

Appropriate Preventive Maintenance Strategy for the Three Equipment Life Cycles

All equipment and buildings require maintenance, and all deteriorate in fairly characteristic ways. Our maintenance and stores systems need to be sophisticated enough to detect where on the critical wear curve we are, and must react accordingly.

1. Start-Up Cycle: Failures occur on materials, workmanship, installation, and/or operator training on new equipment. Frequently the costs are partially covered by equipment warranty. By the nature of this life cycle, there is a lack of historical data. The failures are very hard to predict or plan for, and it is difficult to know which parts to stock.

PM standards are developed in this cycle. Be careful not to weigh the failures in this cycle too heavily because once the machine is understood and is working properly, that failure may never be repeated. This period could last from a day (or less) to several years on a complex system. A new punch press might take a few weeks to get through this cycle, while an automobile assembly line might take 12 months or more to completely shake down. Be vigilant in monitoring misapplication (the wrong machine for the job), inadequate engineering, and manufacturer deficiencies.

Countermeasures to Failure in the Start-Up Cycle (Designed to Shepherd the Asset Through this Cycle and Into Cycle 2):

Enough time to test run equipment

Enough time and resources to properly install

Operator training and participation in startup

Operator and maintenance input into choosing machine

Maintenance and operator inputs to machine design to ensure maintainability

Good vendor relations so they will communicate problems other users have

Good vendor relations so you will be introduced to the engineers behind the scenes

Maintenance person training in the equipment (and periodic retraining when project wears on)

Maintenance person training in startup engineering

Latent defect analysis (run the machine over speed and see what fails, and fix it)

Rebuild or reengineer to your own higher standard

Formal procedures for startup (possibility of videotape).

2. Wealth Cycle: This cycle is where the organization makes money on the useful output of the machine, building, or other asset. This cycle is also called the "use cycle." The goal of PM is to keep the equipment in this cycle or detect when it might make the transition to the breakdown cycle (life cycle 3). After detecting a problem with the machine or asset, a quality-oriented maintenance shop will do everything possible to repair the problem and bring the asset back to the wealth cycle.

After proper startup, the failures in this cycle should be minimal. Operator mistakes, sabotage, and material defects tend to show up in this cycle if the PM system is effective. Also, PM would generate the need for Planned Component Replacement (PCR). The wealth cycle can last from several years to 100 years or more on certain types of equipment. The wealth cycle on a high-speed press might be 5 years, while the same cycle might span 50 years for a low-speed punch press in light service.

Countermeasures to Failure in the Wealth Cycle (Designed to Keep the Asset in this Cycle):

PM system

Operator certification

Periodic operator refresher courses

Close watching during labor strife

Audit maintenance procedures and check assumptions on a periodic basis

Autonomous maintenance standards and quality audits

Quality control charts initiate maintenance service when control limits cannot be held.

3. Breakdown Cycle: This is the cycle that organizations find themselves in when they do not follow good PM practices. Cycle 3 is characterized by wearout failures, breakdowns, corrosion failures, fatigue, downtime, and general headaches. This is a very exciting environment because you never know what is going to break, blow out, smash up, or cause general mayhem. Some organizations manage life cycle 3 very well and make money by having extra machines, low quality requirements, and toleration for headaches. Parts usage changes as you move more deeply into life cycle 3. The parts tend to be bigger, more expensive, and harder to get. The goal of most maintenance operations is to identify when an asset is slipping into life cycle 3 and fix the problem. Fixing the problem will result in the asset moving back to life cycle 2.

Countermeasures to the Breakdown Cycle:

PM system

Maintenance improvement

Reliability engineering

Maintenance engineering

Feedback failure history to PM task lists

Great fire fighting capability

Superior major repair capabilities.

Fig. 13 shows remediation of a problem detected in life cycle 3.

Hold the Presses!

Bad news—PM at its best is only a stopgap. We should be looking at PM as a way station on the road to maintenance improvement. We must eliminate the need for maintenance. The goal of maintenance is to eventually eliminate the need for maintenance departments!

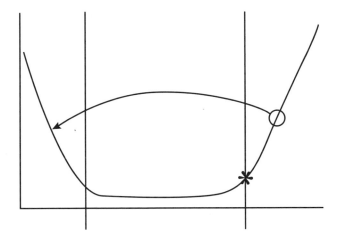

Fig. 13.   Repair in life cycle 3.

The curves in Fig. 14 represent the average life (or MTBF—mean time between failures) of a component such as 1″ bore, 24″ stroke, air cylinder. Left alone, the cylinder will deteriorate and fail in a given amount of time. That is represented by curve A. If you

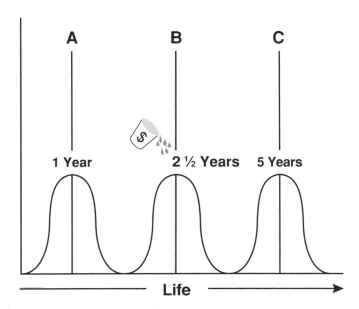

Fig. 14.   The relationship of PM to maintenance improvement.

have more than one, not all of them will fail at once. The curve might look like A. The MTBF will be influenced by how you are using them, how well they are built and engineered, and the conditions under which they operate.

Curve B represents an improved life from PM and predictive maintenance. We are cleaning the cylinders, keeping everything tight, etc. As you notice, the life curve has shifted significantly to the right (showing longer life). To keep the life at this level, funds have to be continuously invested in the form of PM labor and materials. As soon as that flow stops, the curve slides back to A.

Curve C is the goal of maintenance. It is called maintenance improvement, where the life of the unit unattended is longer than either A or B. This could be the result of better seal kits, better cylinders, better protection. We want to increase the MTBF without having to pour money in every month. The maintenance improvement should be logical (we wouldn't spend $50,000 to avoid a $100/month PM effort).

Justifying Preventive Maintenance Expenditures

Some Benefits of a PM System

1. Your inspectors are your eyes and ears into the condition of your equipment. You can use their information on decisions to change your equipment makeup, change specification, or increase availability.

2. Equipment has a breakdown curve: once over the threshold, failures increase rapidly and unpredictably. Working lower on the curve adds predictability and reliability.

3. Early detection avoids core damage and gives you more time to plan and secure parts and specialized tools.

4. Predictability shifts the maintenance workload from emergency fire fighting due to random failures to a more orderly scheduled maintenance system.

5. The frequency of user-detected failures will decrease as the inspectors catch more and more of the problems. Decreased user problems translates into increased satisfaction.

What is the Cost of Breakdown?

One way to sell PM is to discuss the effect of downtime from breakdowns. Breakdowns can be a strong selling point when we develop data on the costs. The following are some costs to consider.

Operator (crew) idle time

Cost of lost production (less material costs)

Cost of rental equipment

Extra travel time for mechanic

Extra repair time due to adverse conditions

Extra costs due to core damage

Extra costs from overtime

Extra damage of associated parts

Extra costs of outside parts and labor

Extra shipping costs

Air freight

Spoilage of product

Disruption to job being interrupted

Disruption to process

Disruption to purchasing

Disruption to storeroom

Damage to morale

Loss of goodwill

Loss of customer

Liability costs

OSHA, EPA fines

Damage to environment

Cost Justification for PM (Will PM Save You Money?)

Add up your average number of breakdowns per year, and compare 70% of that cost to the cost of inspections, adjustment, cleaning, bolting, lubrication, short repairs, and corrective maintenance. (We can assume that 70% of breakdowns will be eliminated through an average-quality PM system.) If the formula below is true for your case, go ahead with a PM system:

$$(\text{number of breakdowns} \cdot \text{average cost per breakdown} \cdot 70\%) > \text{cost of PM system.}$$

The benefits possible from a PM program are real. Getting the benefit of installation of a PM system requires a commitment to the elements of a successful system. In order to maximize the return of your investment in your equipment, it must be kept in peak operating condition. Remember that the PM approach is a long-term approach. Anything less than peak operating condition results in increased operating, maintenance, ownership, or downtime costs. These costs vary slowly. Low overall costs of operation are the result of years of good maintenance policy.

Anyone can reduce maintenance costs for a few quarters by cutting back on PM inspections and the associated repairs. The temptation to do so is sometimes very great because the piper gets paid 1 or 2 years down the road. Because of this temptation and the length of time to get a return on the investment, most organizations have either no PM system or only a partial PM system. Some organizations inspect, lubricate, and adjust, but don't feedback repairs to be scheduled unless there are clear and present dangers. Other organizations use fixed PM task lists with fixed frequencies without any review of failure, histories, or service.

Your management needs to see the longer view regarding proper maintenance—and only you can provide it. Sometimes managers hear from trade conventions or meetings that PM is hot this year, and they use this enthusiasm to help get a program approved or upgraded. Be conservative in your return on investment timing, and liberal on the amount of funds it will take.

Selling PM to Management

The first step is to determine the cost of operating in your current mode. The second step is to prove—through rigorous modeling—that savings or significant improvement to service will result from the proposed improvement.

When possible, include other departments such as production, accounting, or even marketing to help prepare your arguments. A good maintenance effort affects every part of the plant, so every part of the plant has candidates to contribute in your discussions. Marketing is often a good choice because good maintenance will help them with the customers by ensuring delivery dates and maintaining quality.

The end customer may be the strongest voice for PM. For example, all new vendors to General Motors are subject to a plant audit. One of the elements of the audit is to look for the existence of a PM system (that seems to work). GM doesn't want to put its production in the hands of an organization that uses haphazard maintenance practices.

In some cases, maintenance costs might increase, while the overall costs would decrease. The offset would come from decreased downtime, improved customer service, or another area.

Remember that we are in an extremely competitive battle for the organization's investment dollars. Investments in maintenance can earn big returns. We must sell our strong suits, which are cost avoidance, improved customer satisfaction, and reduced downtime. Use the language (and issues) of your organization to sell a PM program. In every organization, there are some issues which are more important than any others.

Benefits of a PM System: The Stakeholder's Priorities

Use these abbreviations to interpret the table below:
Operations/production (O); Maintenance manager (M); Top management (T); Store room (S); Purchasing (P); Engineering (E); Accounting (A).

1. Reduce the size and scale of repairs	M,O
2. Reduce downtime	T,O,E,M
3. Increase accountability for all cash spent	A
4. Reduce number of repairs	M,O
5. Increase equipment's useful life	A,O,E
6. Increase operator, maintenance mechanic, and public safety	O,T
7. Increase consistency and quality of output	O
8. Reduce overtime	A,M
9. Increase equipment availability	O
10. Decrease potential exposure to liability	T,A
11. Reduce backup and standby units	T,A
12. Ensure all parts are used for authorized purposes	S,P
13. Increase control over parts and reduce inventory level	S,P,A
14. Decrease unit part cost	P
15. Improve information available for equipment specification	E
16. Lower overall maintenance costs through better use of labor and materials	M
17. Lower cost/unit (cost per ton of steel, cost per cam shaft, cost per case of soda)	O,T
18. Improve identification of problem areas to know where to focus attention	M,O

Installing Preventive Maintenance Systems

PM Task Lists

The task list consists of the items to be done: inspections, adjustments, lube route, cleaning, bolting, readings, and measurements. Sources of task lists are: manufacturers, trade association recommendations, third-party published shop manuals, your experience, skilled craftspeople, state law, history files with that equipment, review of your records, regulatory agencies (such as EPA, FAA, OSHA, DOD, DOT), consultants, equipment dealers, your customer's requirements, your own engineering department, laws, and insurance companies.

The Four Types of Task Lists (see Fig. 15)

Unit Based: This is the standard type of task list. The worker goes down a list (and completes it) for each asset or unit before going on to the next unit. The mechanic would also correct the minor items with the tools and materials he/she carries (called short repairs). Another variation of unit PM is "gang PM," where several people converge on the same unit at the same time. This method is widely used in utilities, refineries, and other industries with large complex equipment and with histories of single craft skilling. In a TPM-run factory, the operator is responsible for the unit PM. A mechanic might be responsible for an annual, in-depth PM.

Advantages: The mechanic gets to see the big picture; parts can be put in kits, and are available from the storeroom as a unit; person learns the machine well; mechanic has ownership; travel time advantage (only requires one trip); gets into the mindset for the machine; easier to supervise than other methods. Mechanic can discuss the machine with operator as an equal partner.

Disadvantages: High training requirement; higher-level mechanic needed, even for the mundane part of the PM; short repairs can force you behind schedule; if PM is not done, no one else looks at machine.

String Based: This task list is designed to PM one or a few items on many units in a string. Each machine is strung together like beads on a necklace. Lube routes and vibration routes are examples of

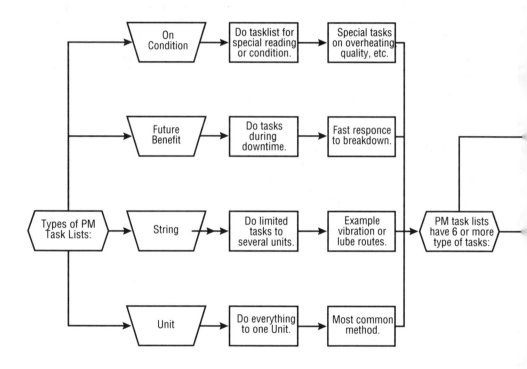

Fig. 15.   PM tasks and task lists.

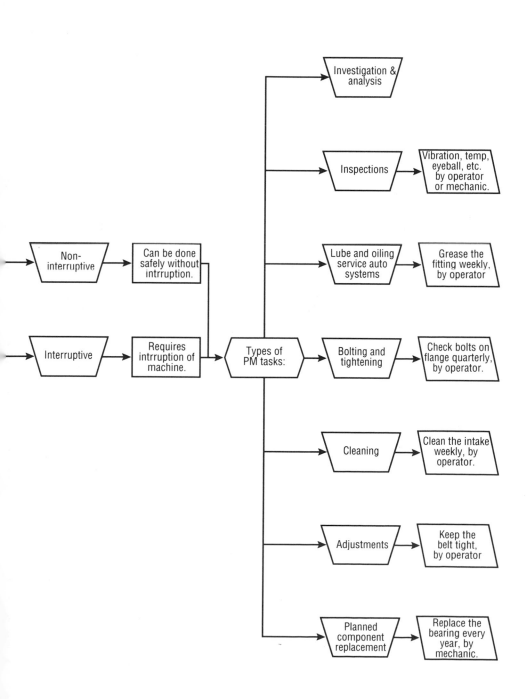

string PM. If the units are located together, it might be easier to look at one item on each unit. The inspector's efficiency would be higher since he/she would be focused on one activity. Most inspection-only PM's are designed this way. Almost all predictive maintenance is handled by various types of strings. Only a few computer systems support string PM and allow a charge to be spread to several assets.

Advantages: Low training requirements; lower level mechanic required; job can be engineered with specific tools and exact parts; route can be optimized; stock room can pull parts for entire string at once; lends itself to just-in-time delivery of parts; easier to set time standards for a string; good training ground to teach new people about the plant; allows new people to get productive quickly.

Disadvantages: Some loss of productivity with extra travel time for several visits to the same machine; don't see the big picture (the string person might ignore something wrong outside the string); boring to do the same thing over and over; no ownership; hard to supervise; if a mistake is made (such as wrong lube), it is spread to all assets on the route quickly.

Future Benefit: This type of task list takes advantage of closely coupled processes. It is commonly considered in the chemical, petroleum, and other process-oriented industries. Since manufacturing is looking more and more like continuous processes, then it will become more popular there also. In future benefit PM, you PM the whole train of components whenever a breakdown or changeover idles one essential unit. It is usually easier to extend downtime for an hour than it is to get a fresh hour for PM purposes.

Advantages: Little or no additional downtime; takes advantage of existing downtime to PM for a future benefit; can become a contest against time; easier to manage; can be exciting.

Disadvantages: Might not have enough people; disruptive to other jobs interrupted when the call comes in; cannot predict when your next PM will be done, so you can plan but not schedule.

Condition-Based PM: The PM service is based on some reading or measurement going beyond a predetermined limit—if a machine cannot hold a tolerance, a boiler pressure gets too high, or a low oil light goes on, a PM routine is initiated. Used with statistical process control to monitor and ensure quality.

Advantages: High probability that some intervention is needed; involves the operator; bring maintenance closer to production; supports quality program.

Disadvantages: Might be too late to avoid breakdown; usually high skill needed; can be planned but cannot be scheduled; many variations are not maintenance problems.

Access to Equipment

One of the most difficult issues of factory operation is access to equipment. Access problems fall into two categories—political and engineering.

Political access problems are problems that stem from political reality. The equipment is not in use 24 hours/7 days—but it is in use whenever you want it for PM. The reason you are not given access might be because production control has assigned no time for the PM, the maintenance department might be distrusted by productions, etc. The following are some ideas for overcoming political access problems.

1. Go back to the planning department to discuss requirements. Do not wait until you need the unit the next day. In some cases, the production schedule might be set weeks ahead of time.

2. Circulate PM success stories from your plant or from the trade press to everyone in production management. Keep doing it until they believe you.

3. Conduct a class in PM and breakdown for operations and production control personnel, with examples of broken parts, and show how PM could have avoided the problem.

4. Use downtime reports now in circulation, and highlight downtime incidents that could have been avoided by PM effort.

5. Use production reports in the same way.

6. Most importantly, conduct yourself with integrity. Give equipment back when promised; show up when promised; if there is a complication, communicate with everyone before, during, and after.

Engineering access problems are easy to spot. These access issues stem from equipment that cannot be taken out of service because it is always in use, e.g., transformers, environmental exhaust fans, single compressors, etc.

A partial antidote for both types of access problems might be *noninterruptive maintenance.*

Interruptive/Noninterruptive: This is a variation on the unit-based theme for machines that run 24 hours a day (or are running whenever you need to PM them). The unit-based list is divided into tasks that can be done safely without interrupting the equipment (readings, vibration analysis, adding oil, etc.), and tasks that require interruption. The tasks can be done at different times. The interruptive list may require half as much downtime as the original task list.

The next step is to reengineer the machine so almost all of the tasks can be done safely without interruption.

Advantages: Same as above, with reduced machine downtime.

Disadvantages: Same as above, except slightly less productive since the machine requires at least two trips.

PM Frequency: How Often Do You Perform the PM Tasks?

PM Frequency and Its Effect on Breakdown

Fig. 16 points out one of the difficulties in planning frequencies of inspection. The key is to minimize total maintenance costs. If the frequency (expense) of the inspections is too high, the total cost goes up. If PM costs are too low, then breakdowns are high and total costs are also high. Each operation has an optimum level of PM activity. What we try to do is continually adjust the frequency and task list to move to the center of the curve (lowest overall cost).

A: The organization at point A has no PM system. All of the

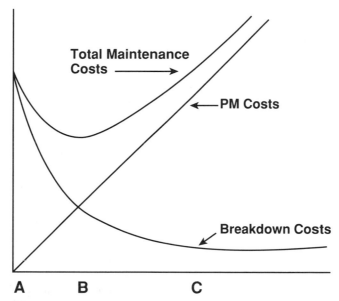

Fig. 16. Total cost of maintenance activity, and effect of increased PM.

maintenance demand comes from users, breakdowns, and routine work.

B: An organization in the B area has balanced its PM system to reflect the original failure rate. This level PM results in the lowest level overall cost for maintenance.

C: The C-level organization has too much PM from strictly a cost point of view. Other factors might drive over-PM'ing, such as government regulations and high liability costs. Airlines and nuclear power plants have both constraints and operate at very high PM levels.

PM Frequency Determination

The first source for inspection frequency is the manufacturer's manual. Ignoring it might jeopardize your warranty. Keep in mind when using the manufacturer and limiting warranty losses. Following that manufacturer's guidelines may mean you will be over-inspecting and over-PM'ing the equipment.

The manufacturer assumptions for how the machine is being used might be different than your usage. For example, one manual recommended a monthly inspection for a machine. When the manufacturer was questioned, it was discovered that the manufacturer assumed single shift use. The factory used the machine around the clock and was getting excessive failures even with recommended PM frequency.

Certain inspections are driven by law (EPA, State, OSHA, DOT). You have a certain amount of flexibility in the timing of these inspections. Consider scheduling them when a PM is also due. While you have the unit under your control, you also perform any routine PM to improve efficiency. Your own history and experience are excellent guides because they include factors for the service that your equipment sees, the experience of your operators, and the level and quality of your maintenance effort.

The PM inspection routines are designed to detect the critical wear point and push it into the future as much as possible. Since we cannot yet see the wear directly, the goal is to find a measure that is easy to use and is more directly proportional to wear. Traditionally, two measures have been used: *utilization* (cycles, tons, miles, hours), and *calendar days.* For almost any measure to be effective, the PM parameter (such as cycles, days, etc.) must be driven from the unit level (unique parameter table for each unit) or from the class level (like units in like service) and have the same PM frequency.

Days: This is the most common method. The PM system is driven from a calendar (e.g., every day, grease the main bearing; every 30 days, replace the filter; etc.).

Advantages: Easiest to schedule, easiest to understand, best for equipment in regular use.

Disadvantages: PM might not reflect how the unit wears out, units might run different hours and require different PM cycles (e.g., one compressor might run 10 hours a week and the other might run 100 hours)

Meter Readings (e.g., change the belts after the compressor runs 5000 hours): One of the most effective methods for equipment used irregularly.

Advantages: Relates well to wear, and is usually easy to understand.

Disadvantages: Has the extra step of collecting readings, and is hard to schedule in advance unless you can predict meter readings.

Use: This is the second most common method. The PM system is initiated from usage such as PM after every 50,000 cases of beverage, or overhaul the engine every 10,000 hours.

Advantages: Utilization numbers are commonly known (How many cases we shipped today). The parameter will be well understood, should be very proportional to wear, not hard to schedule after production schedule is known, harder to calculate labor requirements per month or year.

Disadvantages: Information system might not accept this type of input.

Energy: The PM is initiated when the machine or system consumes a predetermined amount of electricity or fuel. The asset would have a meter or some other method of directly reading energy usage. This is an excellent indirect measure of the wear situation inside the device and the overall utilization of the unit. You probably are already collecting some energy data for other reasons. Energy consumption includes the variability of rough service, operator abuse, and component wear (increased friction). It is used extensively on boilers, construction equipment, and marine engines.

Advantages: Very accurate measure of use in some equipment, and raises consciousness about energy usage.

Disadvantages: Need to wire watt meters or oil meters into all equipment to be monitored. It is hard to schedule ahead of time without a good history.

Consumables (e.g., add-oil; the additions to hydraulic, lubricating, or motor oil are tracked): When the adds exceed a predetermined parameter, then the unit is put on the inspection list. This is a direct measure of the situation inside the engine, hydraulic system, gear train, etc. Wear and condition of seals are directly related to lube consumption.

Advantages: Will alert you if there is a leak.

Disadvantages: Very specialized, very hard to schedule in advance, and hard to collect accurate data.

On-Condition Measures: The PM in this case is generated from the inability of the asset to hold a tolerance or have consistent output. It could also be generated from an abnormal reading or measurement (for example, a low oil light on a generator might initiate a special PM).

Advantages: Responds well to customer needs.

Disadvantages: Almost impossible to schedule, cause is frequently not in the maintenance domain, and might be too late.

Common Tasks

The most common problem is how to choose a task for inclusion on the task list. The general rule is to look at failure modes—how does the asset fail? If you have a history, review all of the modes of failure. Look for three types of failure situations—the modes that are most costly, most dangerous, and most likely. Any task list that follows these three is likely to be effective.

Inspection: This is low tech, high skill application of human senses, including see, feel, smell, hear, taste (only occasionally, such as wine production).

Predictive Maintenance: This is inspection with some help from technology. It could be vibration analysis, infrared scanning, or even megohm readings on a motor winding.

Cleaning: A study by the Japanese Society for Plant Engineering showed that 53% of all breakdowns in factories were caused by dirt and bolting problems.

Bolting/Tightening: Looseness is the second cause for machine breakdown. Bolting includes looseness, missing fasteners, misapplied fasteners, and wrong fasteners.

Operate: On some equipment that is used infrequently, observing the operation is the only way to ensure it will work when needed (e.g., running an emergency generator for an hour each week).

Adjustment: Many components fail because they are allowed to come out of adjustment, such as belts, limit switches, etc.

Take Readings: Many maintenance events follow unusual readings. Other events follow a slow decay in a key parameter that could have been detected by readings, such as boiler failure, air compressor failure, filter changes, etc.

Lubrication: Basic PM includes lubrication. This is a critical item. Training is often slipshod or nonexistent. Investigate automatic oilers which present significant opportunities in this area.

Scheduled Replacement: This is sometimes called planned scheduled replacement. It is used effectively by airlines to produce ultrahigh reliability. It is an excellent (but expensive) tool for mission critical systems.

Interview Operator: Ask questions and build a relationship of mutual respect. The operator is the closest to the action.

Analysis: Review the PM and repair history. Look for areas of possible improvement.

The one ratio always to consider when picking a task is the cost of the task per year related to the cost of the breakdown that is being avoided by this task. Many people design task lists without considering the cost–benefit relationship.

Staffing the PM Effort

"A successful PM program is staffed with sufficient numbers of people whose analytical abilities far exceed those of the typical maintenance mechanic" (from August Kallmeyer, Maintenance Management). We want high level people because they will be able to detect potentially damaging conditions before they actually damage the unit. Your best mechanic is not necessarily your best PM inspector. The key to PM is to choose people who will *do* the jobs rather than people who *say* they will do the jobs. PM is hard to verify (it can be done) and usually boring for the people doing it.

Six Attributes of a Great PM Inspector

1. The individual can work alone without close supervision. The inspector has to be reliable since it is hard to verify that the work was done.

2. The PM inspector is interested in the new, advanced predictive maintenance technology and should be trained in techniques of analysis and in the use of these modern inspection tools.

3. The PM inspector should know how to (and want to) review the unit history and the class history to see specific problems for that unit and for its class. Must be the type of person who will fill out and complete the paperwork.

4. A mechanic is reactive in style. A PM inspector is proactive in style. In other words, the inspector must be able to act on a prediction rather than react to a situation. He/she is primarily a diagnostician, not necessarily a "fixer."

5. The inspector must be highly trained. Some types of critical wear are subtle and difficult to detect. The more competent the inspector, the earlier the deficiency will be detected. The early detection of the problem will allow more time to plan, order materials, and will help prevent core damage.

6. PM inspectors should be full time and separate, if practical, from the rest of the maintenance crew. In some large operations, the PM group receives a pay premium and may have a different style of uniform. In any facility, the PM inspection should represent 10–20% of the hours of the whole crew. If everyone is rotated through the PM crew, ensure that they do PM for a whole day at a time.

Provide the PM inspector with the following tools to perform the tasks.

1. Actual task list with space for readings, reports, observations. Task list should include specs for the completion of the tasks and individualized drawings if indicated. Task list should include appropriate lockout information, confined space entry procedures, and permits.

2. Equipment manual. Inspectors or operators should be encouraged to look through and familiarize themselves with the manuals.

3. Access to unit history files. Every unit should be reviewed annually for trends and opportunities for maintenance improvements.

4. Standard tools and materials for short repairs. Operators should be given the exact tools needed for the PM or cleaning (10 mm wrench, screw gum with 3/16 torx bit, etc.).

5. Any specialized tools or gauges to perform inspection.

6. Standardized PM parts kits, lube, cleaning supplies.

7. Log sheets to write up short repairs.

8. Forms to write up longer jobs.

Strategies to Get PM Done

Every plant has horror stories about machines failing right after a PM. The ongoing challenges of PM are to make sure the work is actually done and to make sure the mechanic doesn't damage the equipment him/herself. Much thought, selling, coaching, and training are necessary to keep the PM crew involved and awake. This positive PM attitude needs the support of management in the form of listening to the inspectors and solving what problems they uncover.

1. In a pulp mill, the supervisor would go through random PM's ahead of time and loosen bolts (nonsafety related, of course) and check them afterwards. Sometimes he or she would make a game of it by telling the mechanic that 10 things were loosened.

2. An electrical supervisor taped "see me" cards inside panels. These cards could be traded for token gifts such as better parking spaces, lunch certificates, extra free time, etc.

3. One of the most interesting methods was the purchase of high-tech tools and training for the PM crew only. Using scanners, computers, and outside services made the PM more interesting and more engaging.

4. Reconfigure PM as a top-level job by including some trouble-shooting, job planning, signoff when complete, safety inspections, and other expanded role activities.

5. Use the string PM for low-skill task list items. Have the PM inspectors supervise the strings.

6. Be sure your plant rewards the uptime rather than for downtime. When asked if they were ever patted on the back or congratulated for machines that didn't break, only a few maintenance professionals could answer affirmatively. Most were rewarded for heroic failures that they worked hard to fix.

Steps to Install a PM (Preventive Maintenance) System

1. Set up the PM task force. The PM task force should be a group that includes craftspeople (I prefer to include the shop steward in union environments, or another opinion leader), one or two staff people (particularly an oldtimer who has seen everything), and someone from data processing (if you are computerizing at this point). In a modern production facility, members of production and production control should be involved on some basis.

2. Analyze the needs and concerns of the maintenance stakeholders. Look at each group and see how they contribute to the success of the organization. Determine who is affected by changes in maintenance. The stakeholders should include, at least: production, production control, stores, plant manager, top management, purchasing, accounting, housekeeping, maintenance craftspeople, maintenance staff (supervisors, planners, clerks), and even outside vendors. Remember that each stakeholder group must be sold individually. Each one has different needs, concerns, fears, and prejudices.

3. Provide the task force with the available resources (people/skills/hours), the required demands (zero-base budget documents), and an analysis of the replacement cost of the asset

being supported. The value of the productive output and its associated factory cost is also useful.

4. Task force set up goals from the system. Objectives are set. At this early point, consider training for members of the task force in computer skills (if you plan on computerizing), like typing DOS, word processors, and spreadsheets. Create daily situations where the newly trained people have to interact with the computer, such as using the word processor or developing spreadsheet templates. This practice is essential at the early stage because you want the task force members to have expertise with computers before computerization of maintenance. Also consider putting in a manual work order system at this point (if you don't have one).

5. After the goals are set, pick a name for the effort. I suggest you stay away from "PM system" as a name since it has negative connotations for nonmaintenance professionals. Some good names might include: PIE (Profit Improvement Effort), DEEP (Downtime Elimination and Education Effort), QIP (Quality Improvement Effort). The name should reflect the goals.

6. Prepare a preliminary budget for the project, and divide the numbers into "setup" and "ongoing", as follows.

Setup:

  A. Modernization of equipment to PM standard (capital costs)
  B. Pay for system to store information
  C. Labor for data collection, data entry
  D. Labor to train inspectors
  E. Labor for task force meeting losses on shop floor
  F. Labor to set up task lists, frequencies, standards
  G. Purchase any predictive maintenance devices
  H Labor to train all mechanics in entry and use of system.

Ongoing:

  A. Labor to carry out PM task lists, short repairs
  B. Parts costs for task lists, PCR's (Planned Component Replacement)

      C. Additional investments in predictive technology

      D. Funds to carry out write-ups (corrective maintenance which will maintain a higher standard of maintenance).

7. Sell PM to each stakeholder by using their needs, concerns, and fears. When approval or sign-off is given, continue to the next steps. If approval is withheld, retrace your steps and reanalyze.

8. Inventory and tag all equipment to be considered for PM. Compile a list of all of the assets (or units) that you are responsible for. If no list exists in plant engineering, start the process with the accounting asset list. This list is a starting point—beware of assets too old and fully depreciated on the accounting list because these assets are the biggest maintenance consumers. Also, the accounting list will aggregate all building systems under "building" rather than breaking it out to electrical distribution system, compressed air piping, etc. See the following section on the plant survey for additional details in conducting the equipment inventory. The list should include the following.

      A. Asset number, brass tag number, or unit number. It should be a unique number.

      B. Make and model of the equipment, if relevant.

      C. Serial number, basic specifications, and capacities.

      D. Physical location.

      E. Financial location (where to change) department, area of responsibility.

      F. Subcomponents of the asset. Include high cost items, especially if they require special skills to support.

9. Select a system to store information about equipment, and select forms for PM-generated work order and check-off sheets. Design the first draft of performance reports, to be revised later, that audit the PM system.

10. Draft an SOP (Standard Operating Procedure) for the PM system. This document will be revised many times before the first year is up. Begin training in the SOP's with the rest of the crew.

11. Task force members or other people from the shop and staff complete data entry or preparation of equipment record cards. Rotate this job so many people have experience. Make sure the SOP truly reflects how to enter new assets (modify as required).

12. Consider temporary workers to replace the task force's hours on the shop floor (and to replace anyone who is rotated through the data entry position). *Important:* Take this opportunity to build critical mass in knowledge of your system by having your people do the data entry.

13. Conduct daily audits of data typed into system. Verify the previous day's entries against the source document or (even better) against the nameplate information on the machine. Rotate the audit job with the data entry job.

14. Select and train people to be inspectors. Allow their input into the next steps. Consider using inspectors to help set up the specifics of the system. Include training in root cause analysis.

15. Determine which units will be under PM and which will be B'n'F (Bust'n'Fix!). Remember that there is a real cost associated with including any item in the PM program. If, for example, you spend time on PM's for inappropriate equipment, you will not have time for the essential equipment. Cost to include in PM Program:

    Cost of Inclusion = Cost per PM * Number of PM per year.

    To decide which units to include in the PM system, apply the following rules to each item.

    A. Would failure endanger the health or safety of employees, the public, or the environment?
    B. Is the inspection required by law or by the insurance company?
    C. How critical is the equipment? Would failure affect quality, stop production, or hinder distribution of products?
    D. Is the capital investment high?

E. Is there spare equipment available, or can the load be easily shifted to other units or work groups?
F. Does the normal life expectancy of the equipment without PM exceed the operating needs? If this is true, PM may be a waste of money.
G. Is the cost of PM greater than the costs of breakdown and downtime? Is the cost to get to (to view or to measure) the critical parts prohibitively expensive?
H. Is the equipment in such bad shape that PM wouldn't help? Would it pay to retire or rebuild the equipment instead of PM?

16. Schedule modernization on units requiring it. Plan to retire bad units if possible. Bad units that are not fixed present big problems for PM systems. It may be better to leave bad units off the system. A bad unit on the system will numb and demoralize the inspectors because they are asked to ignore the problem when it comes up for PM because nothing is done between inspections.

17. Select which PM clocks you will use (days, utilization, energy, add-oil). A clock is designed to indicate wear on a system or asset. Using the number of days elapsed (every 30 days, 90 days, 1 year) is good for assets in regular use. A compressor used irregularly might respond better to run-time hours (PM every 500 hours). A concrete plant might use yards of product (PM every 10,000 yards); a steel mill might use tons of steel.

18. Decide which predictive maintenance technology you will use. Train inspectors in techniques. Even better, provide the information to the inspectors or to the task force and let them pick the modalities.

19. Set up task lists for different levels of PM and different classes. Factor in your specific operating conditions, skill levels, operator's experience, etc. Consider unit based, string based, future benefit based, and both interruptive and noninterruptive techniques. Also consider a pilot program

on a piece of critical equipment. Build your support through publicizing your successes.

20. Be sure the inspectors are well equipped for their jobs. Include basic tools and information listed in the section on "Staffing the PM Effort.".

21. Assign work standards to the task lists for scheduling purposes. Observe some jobs to get an idea of the time required.

22. Engineer the PM tasks. Look at the tasks through the eyes of an industrial engineer. Try to simplify, eliminate, and speed up each task. Improve the tooling and ergonomics of each task.

23. Determine frequencies for the task lists (based on the clocks chosen earlier). Select parameters for the different task lists.

24. Implement system, load schedule, and balance hours. Be sure you predict when the PM hours are going to be needed, and balance these needs to the crew availability. Schedule December and August very lightly. Allow catch-up times.

Survey

The survey is a comprehensive look at all of the maintenance needs of a factory or facility. It is usually organized to travel from room to room, reviewing the asset lists and looking at each entry. Part of the survey is to step back and try to see more subtle or more global maintenance exposures. This annual inspection is relatively detailed and should be planned when you have adequate time.

Write up any observed deficiencies. These deficiencies become scheduled work for the rest of the year. Scheduled work is the least expensive, least troublesome work in maintenance. Almost all deficiencies get worse and some become nightmares given enough time. The key to low maintenance costs is to catch and repair as much as possible before it gets expensive.

If available, attach plot plan or survey (with sizes of the building and lot), aerial photographs, any sets of blueprints or sketches (plan view) showing layout of plant floor, and where utilities enter property and where shutoffs/disconnects are located. Include all asset information sheets. Also include maintenance write-ups for all deficiencies (these write-ups will be placed into the maintenance information system for scheduling). Be sure to look at all potential environmental impacts, including bodies of water, soil contamination, smoke stacks, etc.

The survey process must include a description of each asset, location of asset, and information off the nameplate (serial number, model number, manufacturer, specs). In addition, the following items would be helpful: condition of asset, what work is to be done, and an estimate; replacement value of asset; probability of replacement—immediate, 1,2,3,4,5 years; copy of the owner's manual, parts list, etc.; special conditions that would affect PM; and photographs or videotapes.

Survey the entire facility for maintenance and liability exposure. Be sure to look at the following:

access items such as doors, windows, hatches

ADA requirements (disabled access)

boilers

chemical storage

clean rooms

communication systems, raceways

compressors and air delivery systems, vacuum systems

computer rooms, shop floor computers

control systems (like PLC's, MAP systems)

drain systems, environmentally secure disposal

elevators, people movers

electrical items (major), electrical distribution systems, transformers, substations environmental systems (scrubbers, separators, filters)

environmental inspection (asbestos encapsulation integrity)

food service equipment, kitchen equipment, laundry equipment

exterior finishes, accessories, roofing, roof catwalks, equipment attached to roof, openings

generators, co-gen facilities, power houses

grounds, pavement, sidewalks, parking areas

HVAC components (heating, ventlation, air conditioning) exhaust systems

interior finish, lighting

legal liability inspections such as fire systems, elevators (use contractors?)

mobile equipment, trucks, trains, cranes, ships, cars, pickup trucks, turf equipment

physical structure of building

plumbing items (major), pumps, piping systems, restrooms

production equipment, process equipment

quality inspections, certifications, ISO 9000 requirements

rack systems, automated conveyers, storage/retrieval systems

safety/security systems: fire alarm, fire extinguisher, smoke detectors, security systems

swimming pools, settlement ponds, water intakes

tanks (both underground and above-ground), related piping systems, chemical reactors

trash compactors, trash handling systems, recycling systems

waste, hazmat handling systems.

Inspectors should have the following tools for the initial survey:

binoculars (for visual inspection at a distance)

ASSET INFORMATION SHEET	ASSET NAME:	ASSET NUMBER:
ASSET DESCRIPTION:		DATE
SIZE:		
LOCATION OF ASSET:		
SPECS/ CHARACTERISTICS:		
LOCATION OF DRAWINGS:		
CONDITION OF ASSET:		
WORK TO BE DONE:		
NOTES		
DATE ENTERED:	CHECKED:	SURVEYER:

Fig. 17.   Asset information sheet.

MECHANICAL ASSET INFORMATION SHEET	ASSET NAME:		ASSET NUMBER:
ASSET DESCRIPTION:			DATE:
LOCATION OF ASSET:		DEPT/COST CENTER	
MANUFACTURER:		S/N:	
SPECS/ELECTRICAL CHARACTERISTICS:			
CONNECTED TO ASSET:			
VENDOR:		P.O. #	
OWNERS MANUAL:	DATE IN SERVICE:	ESTIMATED LIFE:	YR
PARTS LIST:	COST: $	SALVAGE VALUE: $	
INSTALLATION BOOK/DWGS:	LOCKOUT INSTRUCTIONS:		
CONDITION OF ASSET: WORK TO BE DONE:			
NOTES:			
DATE ENTERED:	CHECKED:	SURVEYER:	

Fig. 18.   Mechanical asset information sheet.

magnifying glass (to examine paints, surfaces, substrata)

folding knife

instant camera, for recording problems or locations (and access to a good 35 mm and a slide projector)

step ladder

extension ladder

measuring tape

selected hand tools

flashlight.

During an initial survey any deficiencies should be written up on the appropriate asset information form. Survey forms follow (see Figs. 17 and 18).

PM Systems Increase Professionalism

One of the legacies we fight is the old concept of the "grease monkey" mechanic. Through the PM effort and other approaches, we need to increase our professionalism. In other repair fields— such as computer repair and copy machine repair—professionalism is a job requirement.

IMPORTANT NOTE: PM systems fail because *past sins* wreak havoc on any task force trying to change from a fire-fighting operation to a PM operation. Even after running for a few months, there are still so many emergencies that it seems you can't make headway.

You also face unfunded maintenance liabilities. The only way through this jungle is to pay the piper—modernize, and rebuild yourself out of the woods. This is where the investment must be made. Any sale of a PM system to top management must include a nonmaintenance budget line item for past sins to bring the asset base up to the standards. Remember, wealth was removed from the equipment because maintenance funds were not invested to keep it in top operating condition. (See Fig. 19.)

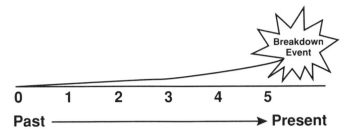

0—No lube, no tightening, no cleaning.

1—First critical wear before detection.

2—Detectable critical wear.

3—Increasingly detectable critical wear.

4—Same as above, only more so.

5—Breakdown event.

Fig. 19.   Historic tail to breakdown events.

Hundreds or thousands of unfunded maintenance liability items are in process at any given time. PM will detect the tail and estimate the time until the catastrophe. The PM discipline will force a repair, rebuild, or replacement.

7.
Predictive Maintenance— Managing Condition-Based Maintenance Technology

Introducing and Managing Predictive Maintenance

The ideal situation in maintenance is to be able to peer inside your components and replace them right before they fail. Technology has been improving significantly in this area. Tools are available that can predict corrosion failure on a transformer; thread through, examine, and videotape boiler tubes; or detect a bearing failure weeks before it happens.

"Scientific application of proven predictive techniques increases equipment reliability and decreases the costs of unexpected failures."[1] Predictive maintenance is a maintenance activity geared toward indicating where a piece of equipment is on the critical wear curve, and predicting its useful life. Any inspection activity on the PM task list is predictive.

Condition-based maintenance is related to predictive maintenance. In condition-based maintenance, the equipment is inspected; and based on a condition, further work or inspections are done. For

[1] Quotation and statistics from J. B. Humphries in an article entitled "Analyzing Predictive Maintenance Needs," in the September 1988 issue of *Maintenance Technology*.

example, in traditional PM, a filter is changed monthly. In condition-based maintenance, the filter is changed when the differential pressure reading exceeds certain readings.

All of the predictive techniques we are going to discuss should be on a PM task list and controlled by the PM system. In this chapter, we will use the common trade press definition of predictive maintenance, which generally refers to technologically driven inspections—in other words, inspections for which you have to buy something (an instrument, scanner, etc.) to perform.

Maintenance has borrowed tools from other fields such as medicine, chemistry, physics, auto racing, and aerospace. These advanced techniques include all types of oil analysis, ferrography, chemical analysis, infrared temperature scanning, magna-flux, vibration analysis, motor testing, ultrasonic imaging, ultrasonic thickness gauging, shock pulse meters, and advanced visual inspection. Most metropolitan locations have service companies to perform these services, or rental companies so you can try some techniques in your facility.

Other instruments not discussed here but which should be considered part of your predictive maintenance tool box are meggers, pyrometers, VOM meters, strain gauges, and temperature-sensitive tapes and chalk. Many techniques and instruments can also be useful in a predictive way because predictive maintenance is an attitude, not a technology! Before you start a predictive maintenance program, consider the following questions.

1. What is our objective for a predictive maintenance program? Do we want to reduce downtime, maintenance costs, or the stock level in the store rooms? What is the most important objective?

2. Are we ready for predictive maintenance?
   A. Do we have piles of data that we already don't have time to look at?
   B. If one of the PM mechanics comes to us asking for a machine to be rebuilt, do we have time to rebuild a machine that is not already broken?
   C. Would production give us downtime on a critical machine on the basis that it might break down?

    D. Are we willing to invest significant time and money in training? Do we have the patience to wait out the long learning curve?

3. Is (are) the specific technique(s) the right technique(s)?
    A. Does the return justify the extra expense?
    B. Do you have existing information systems to handle, store, and act on the reports?
    C. Is it easy and convenient to integrate the predictive activity and information flow with the rest of the PM system?
    D. Is there a less costly technique to get the same information?
    E. Will the technique minimize interference to our users?
    F. Exactly what critical wear are we trying to locate?

4. Is this the right vendor?
    A. Will they train you and your staff?
    B. Do they have an existing relationship with your organization?
    C. Is the equivalent equipment available elsewhere?
    D. In the case of a service company, are they accurate?
    E. How do their prices compare to the value received, to the marketplace?
    F. Can the vendor provide rental equipment (to try before you buy); can they provide a turn-key service giving you reports and hot line service for urgent problems?

5. Is there any other way to handle this instead of purchase?
    A. Can we rent the equipment?
    B. Can we use an outside vendor for the service?

Oil Analysis

One of the most popular techniques to predict current internal condition and impending failures is oil analysis. There are four basic types of oil analysis. They are all related to particle size and composition.

Type	Size	Material
Atomic Emission (AE) Spectrometry	1–10 microns	all materials
Atomic Absorption (AA) Spectrometry	5–35 microns	all materials
Ferrography	20–100 microns	ferrous type only
Chip Detection	40 microns and up	metals only

AE, AA: These two spectrographic techniques are commonly used to look at the whole oil picture. They report all metals and contamination. This is based on the fact that different materials give off different characteristic spectra when burned. The results are expressed in PPT, PPM, or PPB (PPT—parts per thousand, PPM—parts per million, PPB—parts per billion).

The lab or oil vendor usually has baseline data for types of equipment that it frequently analyzes. The concept is to track trace materials over time and determine where they come from. At a particular level, experience will dictate an intervention is required (a rebuild or remanufacture). Oil analysis costs $10 to $25 per analysis. It is frequently included at no charge (or low charge) from your oil supplier.

You are usually given a computer-printed report with a reading of all the materials in the oil and the "normal" readings for those materials. In some cases, the lab might call the results in so that you can finish a unit, or capture a unit before more damage is done. For example, if silicon is found in the oil, then a breach has occurred between the outside and the lubricating systems (frequently silicon contamination comes from sand and dirt). Another example would be an increase from 4 PPT to 6 PPT for bronze, which probably indicates increasing normal bearing wear. This would be tracked and could be noted and checked on the regular inspections.

Oil analysis includes an analysis of the suspended or dissolved non-oil materials including babbitt, chromium, copper, iron, lead, tin, aluminum, cadmium, molybdenum, nickel, silicon, silver, and titanium. In addition to these materials, the analysis will show contamination from acids, dirt/sand, bacteria, fuel, water, plastic, and even leather.

The other aspect of oil analysis is a view of the oil itself. Questions answered include: has the oil broken down? what is the viscosity? are the additives for corrosion protection or cleaning still active?

Consider oil analysis a part of your normal PM cycle. Since oil analysis is relatively inexpensive, also consider doing it: following any overload or unusual stress; if sabotage is suspected; just before purchasing a used unit; after a bulk delivery of lubricant to determine quality, specification, and whether bacteria is present; following a rebuild, to baseline the new equipment, and for quality assurance; and after service with severe weather such as flood, hurricane, or sandstorm.

We have been told stories of two common but simple things to remember with oil analysis. The first is to replace any oil removed for samples. In one large manufacturer, a PM inspector kept forgetting to replace the oil—you can imagine the results! The second common thing is to consider when the oil is being removed. A defense company was doing analysis after oil or filter changes on alternate months. They thought the technique was invalid, because the levels would vary so wildly.

Other tests are carried out on power transformer oil which show the condition of the dielectric, and breakdown properties (a major transformer outage could disrupt your whole facility!).

The first place to begin looking at oil analysis is from you lubricant vendor. If your local distributor is not aware of any programs, contact any of the major oil companies. If you are a very large user of oils and are shopping for a yearly requirement, you might ask for analysis as part of the service. Some vendors will give analysis to their larger customers at little or no cost.

Labs that are unaffiliated with oil companies exist in most major cities, especially cities that serve as manufacturing or transportation centers. Look for a vendor with a hot-line service who will call or fax you in case of an imminent breakdown. These firms will prepare a printout of all of the attributes of your hydraulic, engine, cutting oils, or transmission lubricants. The firm should be able to help you set sampling intervals and train your people in proper techniques of taking the samples.

Tip: Send samples taken at the same time on the same unit to several oil analysis labs. See who agrees, who is the fastest, who has the lowest cost. Pick a lab that maintains your data on computer, and be sure you can get the data on diskette or by modem for analysis.

Wear Particle Analysis, Ferrography, and Chip Detection

These techniques examine the wear particles to see what properties they have. Many of the particles in oil are not wear particles. Wear particle analysis separates the wear particles out and trends them. When the trend shows abnormal wear, then ferrography (microscopic examination of wear particles) is initiated.

Several factors contribute to the usefulness of these techniques. When wear surfaces rub against each other they generate particles. These are normal particles that are benign. The particles generated are divided by size into two groups: small (<10 microns) and large (>10 microns). When abnormal wear occurs, the large particle count dramatically increases. This is the first indication of abnormal wear. After abnormal wear is detected, the particles are examined (ferrography) for metallurgy, type, and shape. These contribute to the analysis of what is wearing and how much life is left.

The most obvious chip detection technology is a magnetic plug in the sump of an engine. You examine the plug to see if dangerous amounts of chips are in the oil. Chip detection is a pass–fail method of large particle analysis. Too many large particles set off an alarm. Several vendors market different types of detectors. One type allows the oil to flow past a low power electrical matrix of fine wires. A large particle will touch two wires and complete the circuit to set off the alarm.

Vibration Analysis

This is a widely used method in plant/machinery maintenance. A recent study of Houston's waste water treatment department showed $3.50 return on investment for every $1.00 spent on vibration monitoring. The same study showed that a private company might get as much as $5.00 return per dollar spent. The study and the vibration monitoring project were done by the engineering firm of Turner, Collie, and Braden of Houston, TX.

Vibration analysis measures the changes in amplitude of the vibration by frequency over time. This amplitude by frequency is plotted on an *XY*-axis chart and is called a signature (also for a given service load). Changes to the vibration signature of a unit means that one of the rotating elements has changed characteristics. These elements include all rotating parts such as shafts, bearings, motors, and power transmission components. Also included are anchors, resonating structures, and indirectly connected equipment.

Many large stationary engines, turbines, and other expensive equipment have vibration transducers built in. The vibration information is fed to the control computer which can shut down the unit or set off an alarm from abnormal vibration. The system also has computer-readable outputs of the data. This allows transfer of the real-time data to the maintenance information system.

Quick Setup of a Vibration Monitoring Program:

1. Buy or rent a portable vibration meter.

2. Train one or more mechanics in its use, make it a regular task on a task list assigned to the same person.

3. Record readings at frequent intervals. Transfer readings to a chart (or use a spreadsheet program and have it do the charting for you).

4. Take readings after installation of new equipment and after rebuilds.

5. Compare periodic readings and review charts to help predict repairs.

6. Do repairs when indicated, do not defer. Note condition of all rotating elements, determine what caused the increase in vibration.

7. Before and after you overhaul a unit, review all vibration readings.

8. As you build a file of success stories, move into more sophisticated full spectrum analysis. Train more widely and trust your conclusions.

Temperature Measurement

Since the beginning of the industrial age, temperature sensing has been an important issue. Friction (or electrical resistance) creates heat. Temperature is the single greatest enemy for lubrication oils and for the power transmission components. Advanced technologies in detection, imaging, and chemistry allow us to use temperature as a diagnostic tool.

Today, there is technology to photograph by heat rather than reflected light. Hotter parts show up as redder (or darker). Changes in heat will graphically display problem areas where wear is taking place or where there is excessive resistance in an electrical circuit. Infrared is unique since it is almost entirely noninterruptive. Most inspections can be safely completed from 10 or more feet away and out of danger.

Readings are taken as part of the PM routine and tracked over time. Failure shows up as a change in temperature. Temperature detection can be achieved by infrared scanning (video technology), still film, pyrometers, thermocouple, other transducers, and heat-sensitive tapes and chalks.

On larger stationary engines, air handlers, boilers, turbines, etc., temperature transducers are included for all major bearings. Some packages include shut-down circuits and alarms if the temperature gets above certain limits.

Possible Uses for Infrared Inspection [2]	Look for
Bearings	Overheating
Boilers	Wall deterioration
Die casting/injection molding equipment	Temperature distribution

[2] This list is from promotional material supplied by Hughes Aircraft Company, Probeye Marketing, Carlsbad, CA.

Distribution panels	Overheating
Dust atmospheres (coal, sawdust)	Spontaneous combustion indications
Furnace tubes	Heating patterns
Heat exchanger	Proper operation
Kilns and furnaces	Refractory breakdown
Motors	Hot bearings
Paper processing	Uneven drying
Polluted waters	Sources of dumping in rivers
Power transmission equipment	Bad connections
Power factor capacitors	Overheating
Presses	Mechanical wear
Steam lines	Clogs or leaks
Switchgear, breakers	Loose or corroded connections
Three phase equipment	Unbalanced load
Thermal sealing, welding, induction heating equipment	Even heating

The following are examples of areas where savings are possible from application of infrared (this information also supplied by Hughes).

- Hot spot on transformer was detected. Repair was scheduled off-shift when the load was not needed, thus avoiding costly and disruptive downtime.

- A percentage of new steam traps which remove air or condensate from steam lines will clog or fail in the first year. Nonfunctioning steam traps can be readily detected and corrected during inspection scans of the steam distribution system. Breakdowns in insulation and small pipe/joint leaks can also be detected during these inspections.

- Hot bearings were isolated in a production line before deterioration had taken place. Replacement was not necessary. Repairs to relieve the condition were scheduled without downtime.

- Roofs with water under the membrane retain heat after the sun goes down. A scan of a leaking roof will show the extent of the pool of water. Sometimes a small repair will secure the roof and extend its life.

- Infrared is an excellent tool for energy conservation. Small leaks, breaches in insulation, and defects in structure are apparent when a building is scanned. The best time to scan a building is during extremes of temperatures (greatest variance between the inside temperature and the outside temperature).

- Furnaces are excellent places to apply infrared because of the cost involved in creating the heat and the cost of keeping it in place. Unnecessary heat losses from breaches to insulation can be easily detected by periodic scans. Instant pictures are available to detect changes to refractory that could be precursors to wall failures.

Ultrasonic Inspection

One of the most exciting technologies is ultrasonic inspection. It is widely used in medicine, and has now moved to factory inspection and maintenance. An ultrasonic transducer transmits high-frequency sound waves and picks up the echo. Echos are caused by changes in the density of the material tested. The echo is timed and the processor of the scanner converts the pulse to useful information such as density changes and distance.

Ultrasonics can determine the thickness of paint, metal, piping, corrosion, and almost any homogeneous material. New thickness gauges will show both a digital thickness and a time-based scope trace. The trace will identify corrosion or erosion with a broken trace showing the full thickness and an irregular back wall. A multiple echo trace shows any internal pits, voids, and occlusions (which cause the multiple echos).

Ultrasonic imaging (the most advanced use of ultrasonics) can create a live image of the inside of the component to be inspected. One interesting application of ultrasound is the shock-pulse meter which reads film thickness of oil on bearings. Based on the film thickness and the bearing number, the operator can read out the likely life of the bearing from a table. Another excellent application of ultrasonic inspection is Bandag's casing analyzer (used for truck tire retreading to detect invisible problems in the casings that could result in failures and blowouts). Since ultrasonics detect changes in density, imperfections in casings are immediately obvious. The transmitter is located inside the casing and 16 ultrasonic pick-ups feed into a monitor. The monitor immediately alerts the operator to flaws in the casing.

A different application of ultrasonics is in the area of ultrasonic detection. Many flows, leaks, bearing noise, air infiltration, and mechanical systems give off ultrasonic sound waves. These waves are highly directional. Portable detectors worn like stereo headphones translate high-frequency sound into sound we can hear, and can quickly locate the source of these noises and increase the efficiency of the diagnosis.

Some organizations enhance this application with ultrasonic generators. This is done by inserting the generator inside a closed system such as refrigeration piping or vacuum chamber and listening all around for the ultrasonic noise. The noise denotes a leak, loose fitting, or other escape route.

Advanced Visual Techniques

The first applications of advanced visual technology used fiber optics. In fiber optics, flexible fibers of very pure glass are bundled together. Each fiber of glass carries a small part of the picture. The smallest fiber optic instruments have diameters of 0.9 mm (0.035″). Some of the instruments can articulate to see the walls of a boiler tube. The focus on some of the advanced models is 1/3″ to infinity. The limitation of fiber optics is length. The longest is about 6′(some are longer). The advantages are cost (about 50% or less of equivalent video technology) and level of technology (they don't require large amounts of training to support).

Another visual technology gaining acceptance is ultrasmall video cameras. These are used for inspection of the interior of large equipment, boiler tubes, and pipelines. These CCD (Charge Coupled Display) devices can be attached to a color monitor through cables (some models used on pipelines can go to 1000′). It uses a miniature television camera smaller than a pencil (about $1/4''$ in diameter and $1''$ long) with a built-in light source. Some models allow small tools to be manipulated at the end, others can snake around obstacles. It is extensively used to inspect pipes and boiler tubes.

The major disadvantages are cost (currently $10,000 to $20,000) and level of support (they require training to adjust and use). The major advantage lies in flexibility. You can replace the heads or cables and end up with several scopes for the price of one.

In most major industrial centers, service companies have been established to do your inspections for a fee. These firms use the latest technology and have highly skilled inspectors. Some of these firms also sell hardware with training. One good method is to try some service companies and settle on one to do inspections, help you choose equipment, and do training. You can also rent most of the equipment.

Magnetic Particle Techniques (Called Eddy Current Testing or Magna-Flux)

Magna-flux is borrowed from racing and racing engine rebuilding, and has begun to be used in industry. This technique induces very high currents into a steel part (frequently used in the automotive field on crank and cam shafts). While the current is being applied, the part is washed by fine, dark-colored magnetic particles (there are both dry and wet systems).

The test shows cracks that are too small to ordinarily be seen by the naked eye, and cracks that end below the surface of the material. Magnetic fields change around cracks and the particles outline the areas. The test was originally used when rebuilding racing engines (to avoid putting a cracked crank shaft into the engine). The high cost of parts and failure can frequently justify the test. The OEM's who build the cranks and cams also use the test as part of their quality assurance process.

Penetrating Dye Testing

Penetrating dye testing is visually similar to Magna-flux. The dye gets drawn into cracks in welded, machined, or fabricated parts. The process was developed to inspect welds. The penetrating dye is drawn into cracks by capillary action. Only cracks that come to the surface are highlighted by this method.

Automated Lubrication Equipment

There has been significant improvement in the reliability of auto lube systems. These systems can now inexpensively be retro-fitted to existing equipment on a one- or multiple-point basis. They provide a level of repeatability and reliability unmatched by most manual systems. The biggest mistake is that organizations forget to add the lubrication equipment to the PM system.

8.
TPM—Total Productive Maintenance

There is a revolution taking place on the factory floor of selected organizations. The ideas of TPM—to make the operator a partner in the maintenance effort—fly in the face of commonly held and cherished beliefs. This import from Japan has taken root in factories, refineries, mills, and power plants throughout North America. It succeeds because it forces us to realize that we have to use more and more of the capabilities of every worker to remain competitive.

In industry, the machine operator is the key player in a TPM environment. There is less reliance on the maintenance department for basic maintenance. Control and responsibility are passed to the operators. In many ways, TPM is a return to a pre-1920's model of maintenance. Before the 1920's, the machine operators were skilled mechanics, so they were expected to repair their own machines. As mass production took over, lower skilled operators were recruited and the production jobs became more menial. Many of these newly minted operators were immigrants or just off the farm. Their greatest asset was the low wages they could be paid and the long hours they worked.

The ability to fix one's own machine quickly disappeared. Training to improve one's skills was nonexistent. Soon this group, as well as management, forgot that these people had capabilities far exceeding their needs as operators. A tradition settled in of operators being only button-pushers. The maintenance department, as we know it, developed at that early time by necessity, with specialists in repairs and maintenance.

A new situation has developed in the way we look at organizations. Throughout the early 1990's, organizations have slimmed ranks, reduced overhead, and optimized processes. At the same time, we also increased the complexity and speed of the equipment and our reliance on computers, PLC's, and sophisticated controllers. We were faced with smaller crew size and greater basic maintenance demands. TPM recruits the operators into the maintenance function to handle basic maintenance tasks and to be the champion of the machine's health. TPM returns to the pre-1920 roots by involving the operator in maintenance activity and decisions. The maintenance department becomes an advisory group to help with training, setting standards, doing major repairs, and consulting on maintenance improvement ideas. Under TPM, maintenance becomes very closely aligned with production. For TPM to work, maintenance knowledge must become disseminated throughout the production hierarchy. The old philosophy to "produce at all costs, damn the torpedoes—full speed ahead" will fall flat on its face with TPM. The operators must have complete, top-level support throughout all phases of the transition and thereafter.

TPM uses the operators (in autonomous groups) to perform all of the routine maintenance including cleaning, bolting, routine adjustments, lubrication, taking readings, start-up/shut-down, and other periodic activities. The maintenance department becomes specialists in major maintenance, major problems, and problems that span several work areas, as well as trainers. The operator goes through seven steps to reach full autonomous maintenance.[1]

1. *Initial cleaning, review of entire machine, tightening.* Complete cleaning of machine. Repair any deficiencies that become apparent during the complete cleaning. Tighten all fasteners to spec. Review entire machine operation.

2. *Maintenance prevention.* Reduce time to perform cleaning. Remove source of contamination. Make the machine easier to service (lubricate, tighten, clean, adjust).

3. *Establish consistent standards.* Specify all tasks and frequencies (daily, weekly, every 1000 pieces, etc.). Set standards for

[1] We would like to acknowledge the groundbreaking work of Nakajima and Suzuki. Much of the information on TPM in this section is derived from the writings of Seiichi Nakajima—*Introduction to TPM* and *TPM Development Program,* published by Productivity Press.

tasks (how clean, what to use to clean, how much and what type lubricant). Autonomous group prepares documentation.

4. *Inspection.* Initial inspection follows manufacturer's manuals, engineering recommendations, and equipment history (what has failed). Group is taught how to correct minor defects.

5. *Autonomous inspection.* Inspection is turned over to group. Check sheets are utilized for all inspections. Minor repairs are completed. Maintenance is only involved in major problems that involve specialized knowledge, skills, or contacts.

6. *Organization to support ongoing TPM.* Systemize the autonomous maintenance activity. Align the organization to support TPM. Use the TPM productivity reports to run the plant. Develop standards for all activity.

7. *Full-functioning TPM.* Track the results of the effort and give ongoing recognition to progress. Monitor failure frequency and look for additional improvements. Spend more time on improvements that reduce maintenance effort while increasing equipment availability.

TPM is one of the most effective methods of improving the delivery of maintenance service while increasing the effectiveness of the equipment. Although in its entirety it doesn't always apply in many situations, certain aspects apply to all maintenance situations. TPM is the maintenance department's answer to the empowerment, job enrichment, and total quality programs on the production floor. The great advantage is that TPM can be incorporated into and can greatly enhance these programs. To begin with, "The dual goal for TPM is zero defects and zero breakdowns" (see footnote 1 again). To achieve this goal, TPM has the following four elements.

- Maximize overall equipment effectiveness. TPM has a very strict definition of effectiveness. One of the tenets of TPM is that sloppy reading of effectiveness can cover up opportunity for production improvement.

- Establish a shared system of PM for the equipment's complete life (take into account the life cycle of the equipment). PM should be modifiable based on the life stage of the equipment. Without this, the PM tasks might not reflect the failure modes of equipment in that condition. The shared PM divides the tasks up between production and maintenance.

• It must be implemented by all departments including maintenance, engineering, and tool/die design operations, etc. Like many other programs of this type, TPM is not really just a maintenance program, but rather a partnership of maintenance and production. The partnership will affect all of the other stakeholders of maintenance. Their involvement is necessary for TPM to thrive. What goes with this is that every employee must be involved in TPM—from the workers on the floor to the president.

• TPM is based on the promotion of PM as a motivational technique through autonomous maintenance groups (operators have greater involvement and say about equipment). TPM works only because the operators begin to "own" the equipment. As ownership spreads, autonomous maintenance becomes a reality.

TPM can be summarized as attention to (and elimination of) the following six losses of production.

Downtime:
1. *Equipment failure from breakdowns.* This is the biggest element which is directly the responsibility of maintenance. With TPM, first line maintenance activity is transferred to operations. Proper design ensures reductions in breakdown-related downtime.

2. *Set-up and adjustment.* The stated goal is single-digit-minute set-up times. This allows up to 9 minutes for set-up. Adjustments are simplified or eliminated from the system. Overall reengineering to reduce these exposures is expected.

Speed Losses:
3. *Idling and minor stoppages due to abnormal operation of sensors, blockage of work on chutes, etc.* These slowdowns are tracked and analyzed to see what is really happening.

Analysis of root causes and of process are ongoing until the system no longer has losses in these areas.

4. *Reduced speed due to discrepancies between design and actual speeds.* Design speeds are reviewed and actual speeds are observed. The comparison, if unfavorable, initiates a design and engineering review.

Defects:
5. *Process defects due to scraps and quality defects to be repaired.* Quality problems are not tolerated. Deep analysis is undertaken until these losses approach zero.

6. *Reduced yield from start-up to stable production.* The production process is tracked and watched for start-up problems. Stable production should follow start-up very closely.

Measuring Equipment Effectiveness is an Essential Part of TPM

Many organizations do not—or cannot—capture accurate information about run time, slowdowns, minor stoppages, and defects. TPM relies on good record keeping in the six areas of loss. The following case study shows the six big losses and a calculation of effectiveness for a manufacturing machine with a 3-second cycle time. Fig. 20 shows all of the variables in calculating effectiveness.

Case Study in Measuring Equipment Effectiveness

Greenfield Manufacturing is one of the leading producers of pipe hangers. They service the electrical and plumbing trades with hangers from ½" EMT to 8" cast iron pipe. They are a single-shift 5-day operation. All machines are shut down for a 30-minute lunch and 15-minute morning startup, and 15-minute evening shutdown periods.

They operate punch presses and small press brakes from 12 to 100 tons in semiautomated to fully automated modes. They have their own tool shop and rebuild presses to their own spec. Automation is a high priority. They use a strategy of minimizing setups by

TPM WORKSHEET FOR EQUIPMENT EFFECTIVENESS   DATE:

SIX BIG LOSSES	MACHINE NAME/NUMBER		DEPT/AREA	
TOTAL TIME IN DAY OR SHIFT	TIME MACHINE NOT RUNNING	EQ	LOADING TIME	
480	60	=	420	

LOADING TIME	LESS	DOWNTIME	EQUALS	OPERATING TIME
420	−	36	=	384

OPERATING TIME	DIVIDED BY	LOADING TIME	EQUALS	AVAILABILITY
384	/	420	=	91.4%

(DESIGN CYCLE TM	x	AMT PRODUCED)	DIVIDED BY	OPERATING TM	EQ	PERF EFFICY
.05	*	6275	/	384	=	81.7%

(AMT PRODUCED	−	DEFECT AMOUNT)	DIVIDED BY	AMT PRODUCED	EQ	RATE OF QUALITY
6275	−	25	/	6275	=	99.6%

OVERALL EQUIPMENT EFFECTIVENESS

AVAILABILITY	*	PERF EFFIC	*	RATE OF QUALITY	* 100	EQ	EFFECTIVENESS
91.4%	*	81.7%	*	99.6%	* 100	=	74.4%

BASIC INFORMATION NEEDED		UNITS
TOTAL TIME IN DAY OR SHIFT	480	MINUTES
TIME MACHINE NOT RUNNING (SCHEDULED)	60	MINUTES/DAY
DOWNTIME FROM SETUP AND BREAKDOWN	36	MINUTES/DAY
DESIGN CYCLE TIME	.05	MINUTES
AMOUNT PRODUCED	6275	PER DAY
DEFECT AMOUNT OF PIECES MADE	25	PIECES/DAY

NOTES TO THIS ANALYSIS:

Fig. 20.   TPM worksheet for equipment effectiveness.

specializing presses so that changes in setup only occur once a week (when they need the press for an unusual size pipe hanger).

This study concerns their new 4″ riser clamp tooling and setup. Four-inch riser clamps are made from 3/16 x 1½″ mild steel. It is shaped with a hump in the middle between 2 ears so that the body of the clamp will hold 4″ cast iron pipe securely and the ears will hold up the pipe at each floor level. The clamp is made on a modified press break in progressive tooling with three stations (form, punch, cutoff). It is fully automated.

The press break (machine number is PB1, located in the heavy metal department) is one of the slowest presses in the entire factory, rated at 20 strokes/minute. In a typical week, there are only 3 hours of downtime from setup and breakdown (36 minutes/day). Average production for the last 30 working days is 6275/day. Since this is a rough-type part, quality problems are few and far between and are usually related to startup, problems in the incoming steel finish, or coil ending losses. They estimate average reject rates from all sources to be 25 pieces per day.

Please note calculations for the overall equipment effectiveness; compare these results to TPM standards:

Availability	>90%
Performance efficiency	>95%
Rate of quality parts	>99%

Installation of TPM

The following three basic requirements prepare the soil for the transplantation of TPM concepts and attitudes.

Motivation: The whole staff and all the workers need to be open to a change of attitude toward waste. This takes place over a long period of time as organizations present, train, and start to change toward TPM.

Competency: Certain skills are necessary before TPM can succeed. Training operators in PM, and training design engineers and mechanics in root failure analysis, will eliminate waste and losses.

Fig. 21.   TPM typical specification for maintenance work.

Environment: The thrust for improvement must be supported by the top managers in the organization. The top people must understand the need for (and the implementation of) TPM.

Any implementation of TPM has to face real problems. Following the plans already mentioned will minimize the negative effects. At a TPM seminar recently, supervisors were asked what real problems they would encounter installing TPM. These problems must be thought about, discussed, and overcome to have an effective TPM effort.

- Top management should give signoff and support throughout a multiyear TPM process. If your management has a short view, they might agree to a multiyear plan and withdraw their support after the first year.

- Top management might give lip service but does not support it with their deeper commitment and their time. How do we get top management to be boosters of the program?

- Supervisors might criticize rather than solve problems, they also might complain and doubt the success of the project in front of their subordinates.

- TPM requires minimal downtime. How do you integrate TPM with customer demands and the sometimes unreal demands of the forecast and production schedule?

- The workers might object to the perceived "extra" work by a slowdown, increases in absenteeism, letting quality suffer, etc.

- Where does an organization (small, medium, large) get time to do all the training necessary?

- How do you run TPM in a high turnover situation? Operators don't stick around long enough to get trained.

- Where do temps fit into TPM? We use temps to operate machines during busy times.

- How do you solve the problem of inadequate communication between the production group and the maintenance group? Who will really manage the maintenance part of the operator's job? Why should operations take advice about operator maintenance effort after TPM when they won't *now?*

- Is there willingness and is there interest to accept the new roles of the two groups?

- Operators don't like to clean equipment and neither do maintenance people.

- Where do our die setters (setup people) fit into this scheme?

"Total Productive Maintenance (TPM) is indispensable to sustain just-in-time operations," says Dr. Tokutaro Suzuki, senior executive vice president of the Japan Institute of Plant Maintenance. In a JIT system, he emphasizes, "you have to have trouble-free equipment." Prior to the adoption of TPM, Japanese manufacturers found it necessary to carry extra WIP inventory "so the entire line didn't have to stop whenever equipment trouble occurred."[2]

Dr. Suzuki defines TPM as "preventive maintenance with total participation." Rather than relying entirely on a staff of maintenance specialists to keep equipment in good running order, TPM pushes the responsibility down to the people operating the equipment. "The concept is that the operator must protect his own equipment," he explains. "Thus the operator must acquire maintenance skills." However, maintenance experts may still make periodic inspections and handle major repairs. And design engineers also play a big role. They must take maintenance requirements—and the cost of equip-

[2] Information about the originator of TPM, excerpted from an article titled "Lessons from the Guru's," published in *Industry Week,* August 6, 1990.

ment failure—into consideration when they design the equipment, stresses Dr. Suzuki.

Even in a non-JIT environment, TPM can yield impressive benefits, the JIPM executive says, by reducing losses associated with machine downtime, product defects, and low yields. The goal, simply, is to "maximize the total efficiency" of production equipment. In one Japanese plant, adoption of TPM reduced the number of equipment failures by 97%. In other cases cited by Dr. Suzuki, TPM boosted labor productivity by 42% and reduced losses related to downtime by 69%.

9.
Where Does Maintenance Fit In?

The maintenance department interfaces with purchasing, stores, traffic, and accounting in addition to production. This section explains the point of view of these departments and their relationship to maintenance, and how they effectively work together. Never forget that the goal of each department is the increased long-term profit of the organization. Each function approaches this goal with differing assumptions, tools, and world views.

Accounting Department

The accounting department is frequently the center of the belief that maintenance is a necessary evil. Certainly any changes in the way maintenance is delivered will face the accounting hurdle: does this change, transformation, reevaluation make financial sense? This is a group of professional disbelievers; accounting should be totally profit and numbers driven. Some business texts say that the accounting department is the score keeper of the business game. Their role actually goes far beyond score keeping because in many areas the accountants are on the field producing profits. In all organizations, the accounting department is the guardian and final arbitrator of what is profitable and what is not.

One continual issue is that, in the eyes of accounting, maintenance is a pure expense—a necessary evil, if you will. In the general ledger (the bible of accounting for your organization), expenses reduce profit, and anything that reduces profit is bad. Unless we create a different view, we can never be anything else to the accountants.

In addition to their gate keeper role, the accountants categorize every financial transaction that takes place in the organization. This categorization is essential to determine profit or loss. Maintenance departments are frequently on the cutting edge of these decisions. For example, many accounting discussions deal with the decision to capitalize or expense for a major repair. In one case, the repair is an investment in the organization and becomes an increase in the value of an asset; in another case, the same repair is an expense, i.e., a nail in the coffin of profit. Another complication in the relationship is the difficulty of coming up with hard numbers for maintenance investments. We could have a clear improvement that is almost impossible to prove with hard numbers.

The accounting department uses double-entry book keeping techniques. That means that every transaction has two sides. A parts purchase will increase A/P (accounts payable—what is owed) when the invoice is posted, and will also increase the expense account. When a machine is purchased, the invoice is booked to A/P and also to an asset account. (See Fig. 22.)

All maintenance work must be accounted for within the general ledger (GL). The accounts mentioned above (expense, asset, A/P) are accounts in the general ledger. The GL is the score card of the organization that reports the condition of the finances, profitability, assets, and liabilities. A repair to a machine is fundamentally different from a rebuild/improvement to the same machine. These different types of transactions must be differentiated and reported. The following are some categories Accounting might be tracking:

maintenance materials such as pumps, repair parts

maintenance supplies such as rags, absorbent pigs

contract labor

maintenance labor, fringe benefits, overtime

labor and materials for grounds

housekeeping services

maintenance support like supervisors, staff, manager

costs to fabricate tools, jigs fixtures, whole machines

nonrecurrent labor on large repair jobs

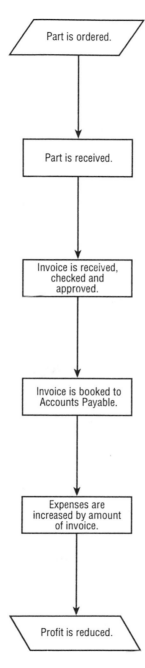

Fig. 22.   How parts are charged against the books.

structural repairs to building

contractor charges on large repair jobs (over $50,000).

The accounting department also verifies that the transaction doesn't exceed any of the predetermined limits (if limits are exceeded, then special authorization might be needed). Example amounts that a maintenance department of a large manufacturer can spend without special authorization are as follows:

Type of Charge	Limit Before Higher Authorization is Needed
Office furniture	$500
Computers, instruments	$1000
Small tool purchase	$500
Capital spares program purchase	$5000
Any MWO eligible for capitalization	$5000
$ limit on any individual MWO	$40,000

Costs need to be charged to the department that incurred them. This tracking and charging all costs is the function of the cost accounting group within accounting. It is difficult to divide maintenance up into maintenance costs per product line since some costs span several products.

Cost accounting is one of the most complex functions of the accounting profession. Cost accounting determines the factory cost of each product line. To do cost accounting correctly, overheads (such as energy and phone, and support departments such as maintenance, purchasing, receiving, etc.) must be allocated to the most logical product. For example, a plant that manufactures wire harnesses uses injection molding equipment which uses large amounts of energy. In fact, the molding department might use $1/2$ or $2/3$ of all the electricity consumed by the whole plant. Cost accounting might calculate this and add the additional overhead to the cost of each plug molded. This more fairly assigns costs to products.

Many fights are the result of illogical or incorrect assignments of overhead. A low-tech division of an aerospace company was stuck with the burden rate of the entire company (which made it competitive in aerospace but noncompetitive in the low-tech area.) They could not convince the accounting management that the sophisticated engineering, computerization, and other elements of aerospace made no sense in the low-tech arena.

Chargeout Rate: Accounting also maintains chargeout rates for all job classifications. The chargeout rate includes hourly wages, fringes (retirement costs, insurance, FICA, vacations, etc.), and overhead (supervision, clerical costs). This number is important because it is the comparison number for outside contractors bidding jobs against inside people.

Accounting and the Maintenance Parts Inventory: The hardest thing to remember is the fact that the maintenance stores do not exist as an asset of the organization by the rules of accounting. Since all financial transactions in the organization follow the rules of double-entry book keeping, let's trace two different store room transactions.

Raw Material Purchase:

1. Raw materials come in the door, invoice comes in the mail.

2. Invoice is booked to accounts payable (a liability account), raw materials are booked to raw materials (an asset account).

3. Invoice is paid, which is booked to the cash account (reducing an asset), while accounts payable is reduced by the same amount.

4. The result is that the asset cash is traded for the asset raw materials.

5. No effect on profit until the raw material is used and the product is completed and shipped to the customer or the warehouse.

Maintenance Parts Purchase:

1. Maintenance parts come in the door, invoice comes in the mail.

2. Invoice is booked to accounts payable (a liability account), maintenance parts are booked to expenses, maintenance parts (an expense account) profit is reduced immediately.

3. Invoice is paid, which is booked to the cash account (reducing an asset), while accounts payable is reduced by the same amount.

4. The result is that the asset cash is consumed by an expense.

5. Profit is reduced when the item comes in the door in step 2.

6. The item might be sitting on the shelf in the store room, but there is no asset on the books.

When the organization needs more cash or additional profit, one place to look is the maintenance parts in the store room. These parts are an asset that does not appear in the books. Metaphorically speaking, if you squeeze the store room, profit and cash drip out! This explains the zeal with which the maintenance stock is attacked.

Effective Arguments to Use with Accounting

Savings Acceleration: Maintenance savings flow directly to the bottom line. The profit of a typical organization is 5–10¢ for every dollar of revenue. A dollar of maintenance cost avoidance or cost reduction is worth $10–$20 of revenue.

Cost Reduction: The maintenance budget was $7,000,000 last year and will be $6,500,000 this year with these changes.

Cost Avoidance: At the rate of deterioration, our costs will go up $500,000 next year unless we take these steps.

Cost Control: The maintenance effort cash needs varied by 50% month to month for the last 3 years. With these changes, we will be able to predict the cash needs to plus or minus 10%.

Increased Production by Increasing the Availability of Assets: We achieved 7950 hours of production last year on the big widget line. With these modifications and changes, we will run 8220 hours next year.

Insurance Policy as a Model for Capital Spares: The failure of any of the 30 parts on this list could shut down production for at least 4 weeks, and probably as much as 12 weeks. We lose

$1,000,000 of direct revenue each week we are out of production. We currently stock only 5 of these parts. For an investment of $375,000, we could stock the rest of the parts and ensure the uptime against catastrophe.

Maintenance has impacts throughout the organization. Its impact affects the entire cost structure of your product. When talking to the accounting department, specific causes and effects must be mapped. Look for costs outside the normal maintenance area for persuasive arguments.

Cost areas to discuss are:

maintenance parts, labor, contract labor, service contracts

energy cost (including electricity, gas, oil, coal)

water costs

cost of shorter equipment life

cost of downtime

cost of scrap

cost of poor quality (variation in the process)

cost of accidents—medical, lost time, legal

cost of environment fines

cost of lowered productivity.

Purchasing

The purchasing department's mission is to buy (at the lowest cost) the materials (that meet the specifications) necessary for the business. In addition, purchasing is usually involved in contractor negotiation, new machine procurement, and is sometimes in control of the store room.

Maintenance is a headache for most purchasing departments. Maintenance demands make it very difficult to implement continuous improvement in purchasing. The needs of maintenance are at odds with some of the methods usually used for improvement in purchasing.

Continuous Improvement Technique	Maintenance Reality
Reduce the number of vendors	100's of vendors
Become a big customer for better service	Small buys
Planned purchases	Unplanned events
Consolidate buys, blanket orders	Uneven requirements
Take time to do it right, the first time	No time, rush, ASAP
Time for low-cost shipment	Air freight, courier required
Maintain quiet, efficient atmosphere	Crazy, emergency room atmosphere

The purchasing department is one of the major interfaces to the outside world. It is also is charged with the mission to protect the organization from certain types of lawsuits and fraud. All organizations are regulated by a series of commerce laws called the UCC (Uniform Commercial Code) which regulate commerce. Additional coordination responsibilities are added when the firm is a JIT (Just-In-Time) manufacturer.

Every dollar saved by purchasing flows to profit. In some organizations, the major portion of funds are spent by purchasing for raw materials and supplies. This direct relationship to profit sensitizes purchasing agents to saving money. Losing control of even dimes and quarters can affect profit by thousands of dollars at the end of the year. Unlike the maintenance department that labors without oversight and whose actions are evaluated indirectly, the actions (or inactions) of purchasing are sometimes painfully visible to accounting and organization management.

The main technique used to get the best price, specification, and delivery is shopping and contract negotiation. Because of the requirements from the organization's auditors and legal counsel, the preference is to shop around and get bids from several sources. In public agencies, this process is required by law. In most factories it is strongly recommended by customs and regulations. Fair shopping is the best protection the purchasing agent has against charges of fraud, collusion with vendors, and other malfeasance.

As a result of shopping around, the purchasing process takes time. Preparation, workload, complexity of the buy, experience, and quality of history files all impact the time it takes to issue a purchase order (PO). To a maintenance professional, doggedly shopping each part looks like a waste of time. Shopping is good purchasing practice. Good mechanics will not necessarily fix the first thing they see until they understand why the failure occurred. That is good maintenance practice—it takes a little longer, but in the long run makes sense.

The other problem that seems to occur with regularity is that the maintenance planner or supervisor locates a part needed. To locate the part, they work with a vendor (who might put significant time into the research). The requisition, with all of the research and the vendor recommendation, is sent to purchasing. Purchasing seems to ignore the recommendation and buys the part from another vendor. This is an unfortunate communication problem. Meetings with the purchasing agent and other managers should include discussion and determination policy in these situations. Sometimes the value added is worth the higher price, and sometimes it amounts to a sweetheart deal for the vendor.

Consider the following example. In the purchasing department of a metal producer, over 13,000 purchase orders are issued in a typical year. In the recent downsizing, their staff was halved. Their reaction, which will be hailed by maintenance departments, was to set up 30 prime maintenance vendors and several thousand commonly used items. They called these items "E" items. These vendors had prenegotiated blanket contracts for "E" items from these vendors. They had a limit of $500 per line item.

The move toward JIT adds to the complexity of the purchasing mission, and increases the stakes. Traditionally, buffer stocks insulated the factory (and the purchasing department) from costly stockouts of critical raw materials. JIT techniques eliminated the buffers. Now when delivery problems arise, purchasing is on the front lines to contribute to solving any problems.

When talking to maintenance managers, one constantly hears stories about the purchasing department buying junk to save a few dollars. Purchasing uses specifications prepared by engineering, production, and maintenance to determine what it buys. Specifications are detailed descriptions of the qualities, performance, and function of the item purchased. Usually these mistakes are traceable to the specifications being incomplete or incorrect. Purchasing is totally dependent on the completeness and accuracy of the specifications; they cannot independently judge the qualities of the parts or supplies purchased.

Over the years, organizations make mistakes and learn which things to avoid. The purchasing department (in conjunction with legal counsel) keeps track of this information in its "Terms of Purchase" (which are usually printed on the back of the PO). Some typical terms, and what they are designed to protect from, are as follows.

Acceptance: The PO sent to the vendor is just an offer to purchase. The vendor has to acknowledge the PO or act as though they accept, by shipping the order, for example. The PO is not tied to a quote or bid by the vendor, but is an offer that they can accept or reject. In legal terms, acceptance actually forms an enforceable contract. It is important to know when and if the PO was accepted.

Changes: These must be agreed to in writing in order to be binding. Verbal changes are the subject of a large portion of lawsuits with vendors. This protects both organizations.

Force Majeure: Either party can be excused from performance by acts of God, fires, labor disputes, acts of government, and a whole list of possible problems. After a catastrophe, the last thing you need is a flurry of lawsuits for undelivered parts.

Design Responsibility: The seller is totally responsible for the design of the product. The PO is a request to meet specifications, not a design of a product. If the design is defective, this places the blame on the vendor and protects your organization from certain liabilities.

Warranties: Any products bought by PO are warranted by the vendor as fit for the intended purpose and should be free from defects. Seller is to fix, replace defective items, or refund all money including shipping charges. Products should do what they are supposed to do, and if not you can return them.

Intellectual Property Rights: The seller owns the rights to the product it is selling. The seller is not infringing on anyone else's patents or licenses. This protects you against the suit where the vendor is in a dispute with a third party about patent ownership of the item purchased. Some third parties might sue you if the purchase is large enough.

Confidentiality: Any information given to the seller, or anything developed by the seller for you, is confidential. This confidentiality lasts for x number of years. You might have to tell a vendor a trade secret or show them a proprietary process so that they can help you. This alerts them to keep the secret. Where critical secrets are revealed, stronger nondisclosure agreements are usually required.

Termination: For stock items, you can cancel the order and only pay for items shipped. For a custom-made item, you will pay for only the work accomplished. Certain overhead and profit might be paid after negotiation. Termination before completion of an order is always a sticky affair. This limits your liability.

Indemnity: Except for negligence on your part, the seller indemnifies (protects) you from any damage (lawsuits) brought as a result of the purchase. If a batch of chemicals you purchase explodes while being mixed at the vendor's facility, you are protected by the vendor from being held liable.

Assignments and Subcontracts: A PO cannot be assigned or the work subcontracted without written consent. You want to know who is actually doing the work.

Delivery: The promised date is important (time is of the essence). If a vendor fails to deliver in the specified time, you can cancel the order without any damages, or you can buy the product from another vendor and charge the first vendor the difference. For some items delivery time is critical. This alerts the vendor that you can get damages from them if they miss deliveries.

Price Warranty: The seller warrants that the price charged is the best price charged to any customer for this volume. Price shown on the PO is complete, and there are no hidden charges, this keeps the vendor from charging you a higher price than anyone else buying that quantity. Hidden charges have to be revealed to be acceptable.

Default: If the vendor breaks any of the rules, you can break the contract without any additional charges. This is a legal device to allow you the greatest flexibility to cancel if the vendor breaks any rule.

The following are some ideas to improve the purchasing–maintenance relationship.

- After an emergency is over, invite the purchasing agent or buyer into the shop to show them what was bought. Frequently a $35 solenoid is very impressive when actuating a $700,000 machine which generates $48,000 a day.

- Give time when possible. Many emergencies are due to a lack of planning on your part. Work on getting the maintenance act together to reduce the number of unscheduled events.

- When you or your staff does research into a vendor for a part, pass along your work but do not expect that it will be followed exactly.

- Look closely at specifications on items that have been giving you trouble. It is possible that your problem is in the specs and not in the purchasing department.

- Humanize the relationship by finding out about the people in purchasing. Find out what makes them tick and what pressures they face.

- In larger departments, try to negotiate a specialist to handle the bulk of the maintenance buys. In the best cases, the specialist can be moved to the maintenance department.

Saving Money in Maintenance Purchases

To analyze inventory, sort each part number by dollar volume (unit price times yearly usage). In one study, it was determined that the top 7% of the line items represented about 75% of the yearly purchase volume. These high-cost and fast-moving items are called the "A" items.

- Consider dividing your inventory into "A" items and other items.

- Apply rigorous purchasing and negotiating techniques to "A" items to lower costs. This is an excellent application for the skills of the purchasing department.

- Review specifications to get better parts at the same costs or equivalent parts at lower costs. This is the situation where some level of engineering can pay off in big returns. Areas to look at can include lubricants, bearings, wear parts, fittings, belts, fasteners, wiring/electrical.

- Apply sophisticated standards to setting reorder point and economic order quantity. Factory production inventory control experts have long studied inventory strategies. The "A" level items respond best to these techniques.

- Consider creative new vendors, purchasing modes, and approaches (such as: instead of purchasing fasteners from industrial vendors, go directly to screw jobbers or manufacturers). Another significant savings is to install tanks for high-volume oil to purchase truckloads.

- While not a savings for purchasing, these "A" items also represent most of your labor. Any successful attempt to reduce the need for these parts will also reduce the need for your labor. In other words, the "A" items are the best indicators of opportunity for maintenance improvement.

Stores

The primary reason for a maintenance inventory is to help increase uptime and higher production. Keep in mind that 40–60% of all maintenance dollars flow through the store room. The store room can save the organization significant amounts of money by investing as little as possible in an inventory that supports maintenance. They can also help improve productivity by being able to find any part in stock within a few minutes.

The store room takes heat if there is too much stock (from management), too little stock (from maintenance and production), if a part is not in stock that is on the computer (from maintenance, auditors, and production), if it takes too long to find parts (from the mechanics), or if anything else goes wrong. Next to purchasing, the store room is the most complained about department servicing maintenance.

Types of Inventories[1]

The most common type of inventory is a resale inventory. In this model, money is made by turning over the inventory through sales. The goal is to have exactly the amount of inventory that your customers want. The ruling ratio is turns of inventory per year. In stores they also look at sales per square foot (I have not heard of anyone applying this to maintenance—yet!).

Another type of inventory is the production inventory. This inventory consists of raw materials that are consumed by the production process. The production flow is the most important issue. The measure is in days (or hours) of stock and work in process. The goal is zero. The advances in this area have caused problems in maintenance. JIT (Just-In-Time) works well in production where you can predict the needs of the process. It creates a problem because there is no buffer if a machine breaks down. JIT usually requires an increase in the maintenance stock level.

The type of inventory we deal with in our stock rooms is in support of productive assets. The goal is to be able to ensure equipment availability. We want to keep the minimum stock level that will support the equipment. Of course, we want to set up valued vendor programs to lower stock. We also want to keep the money invested as low as possible. The goal is production. The measure should be lowest downtime due to parts.

[1] *Maintenance Management,* by Jay Butler, published by University Seminar Center (address in the Resource section).

Functions of the Store Room

Administration:

Providing information to the planner or supervisor

Doing all of the calculations associated with stock keeping (min, max, EOQ, safety stock)

Maintaining the parts numbering system

Creating and maintaining a parts catalog

Preparing reports for management

Tracking parts to and from rebuilders

Accounting for all parts received, used, and left on hand

Receiving:

Unloading trucks

Counting parts

Inspecting parts for compliance with specifications

Facilitating quality efforts

Checking for correct part numbers

Verifying PO exists and detailing match packing slips

Providing proof of receipt to accounting to pay vendors

Storage:

Putting away parts

Storing without damage

Rotating stock

Providing security against theft and vandalism

Counting parts (physical inventory)

Maintenance Support:

Reserving (putting aside) parts for jobs

Building kits with parts, supplies, and possibly tools for common jobs

Pulling parts for jobs off shelves and preparing them for transportation (pick-up)

Locate parts

Helping with research into infrequently used parts

Identifying unknown, broken parts

Traditional Problem Areas to Address:

Hoarding of parts by craftspeople

Field reengineering (with no documentation)

Inadequate storage

Slow parts window

Inflexible and hard to use computer system for inquiry and research

Inadequate tracking and staging of parts coming from and going to rebuilders

No physical inventory taken, all kinds of stuff in the inventory

No one wants to write off bad or obsolete stock and take the hit

Bad relationship between stores and the tradespeople

No ability to add to the stock list

Three Categories of Part Uses

Usage-Driven Parts: Simplest type of part to understand, parts that wear out (belts, bearings, wear parts). You use the part because it wears out. If your production goes up, usage of these parts usually increases somewhat in step. If production goes down, then usage eventually goes down. If you get a slew of novice operators, then these part usages increase until everyone is trained. This type of part is usually well understood by management outside maintenance. This type of usage responds well to retail inventory analysis such as evaluating by TURNS or EOQ.

Paperwork-Driven Parts: Parts used for construction, PM, and PCR parts. Usage is driven by a number on a drawing or a study of paperwork. The problem is that any change in the paperwork immediately changes the part needs. This type of part can be disruptive to a stock keeping system because the usage can wildly change as the paperwork is modified. For example, look at the impact of a large construction job on EOQ (annual usage will be artificially inflated).

Fear-Driven Parts: Parts that have long leadtime and are hard to duplicate for high downtime cost machines or processes. These parts support mission critical machines. They may come from overseas. In a power utility these parts are called capital spares. They are handled differently on the books. When a new plant is built, spare parts are purchased and depreciated with the machines where they arc used. Another name is insurance policy parts. These parts are an insurance policy against downtime. Like insurance policies they have premiums (the cost of the part and carrying cost of the store room) and benefits (avoided downtime). The fear-driven parts do not respond to the retail model and tend to confuse conventional inventory analysis. Remember, the fear parts are on the shelf (just like your fire insurance policy)—to *not* use. In fact, using your insurance parts is usually indicative of a breakdown in your PM system.

Primer on Maintenance Store Keeping[2]

The Retail Model of Store Keeping: This model says that every item that does not move in a given period of time should be removed from the shelf and eliminated. In a retail store, every square foot of shelf space is evaluated for its productivity. If something

[2] Some elements of the formulas were adapted from *The Production Managers Handbook of Formulas and Tables* by Lewis Zeyher, published by Prentice-Hall in 1972.

doesn't move, then it should be replaced by something that will. Some of the formulas and ideas below are borrowed from this model. It is important to identify which ideas work in maintenance and which ones are deadly. New models are needed for certain classes of parts.

How to Conduct a Physical Inventory: There are two methods of conducting a physical inventory. The old method is annual physical inventory where the department shuts down for one or more days and physically counts everything. Newer methods use cycle counting strategies. This means that 1/12 of the inventory is counted every month. In a year, all of the parts are physically counted. The advantage of cycle counting is that there is no shutdown necessary. It can also be accomplished with existing staff during slack periods. You also have a great deal more flexibility with cycle counting if you start having stockouts. In addition to cycle counting, the counts are updated whenever there is a stock outage.

How to Calculate a Safety Stock: The safety stock is the difference between your average usage of a part and the maximum probable usage of that part for a period equal to the leadtime.

$$\text{Safe} = (Um - Ua) \cdot L$$

where Um = the maximum probable usage for that part per week, Ua = the average or usual usage for that part per week, and L = the leadtime in weeks. For example, the safety stock for a part where 12 is the average usage and 18 is the peak usage and a 4 week leadtime would be: $(18 - 12) \cdot 4 = 24$.

How to Calculate the Minimum: The minimum stock level is the least amount of stock you want to have on the shelf. In theory, your stock level should fall to the minimum on the day the truck brings your reorder. In a JIT shop, the minimum is zero.

$$\text{Min} = (U \cdot L) + S$$

where U = average usage of the part per week, L = leadtime for that part in weeks, and S = safety stock. For example, using the above example, the average usage is 12 and the leadtime is 4 weeks. We calculated the safety stock parts: $(12 \cdot 4) + 24 = 72$.

How to Determine the Reorder Point: We want to reorder so

that when the order comes in, our stock level has dropped to the minimum.

R.O.P. $= (U \cdot L) + \text{Min}$

where U = average usage of the part per week, L = leadtime for that part in weeks, and Min = minimum inventory level. For example, using the above situation, the usage remains at 12 per week and the leadtime is still 4 weeks. The reorder point is calculated as follows: $(12 \cdot 4) + 72 = 120$.

How to Calculate the E.O.Q. (Economical Order Quantity): The economical order quantity is the amount to place on order at one time. This is an area where the thought is changing regarding the use of blanket orders to lower processing costs. This formula gets significantly more complex when the unit price varies with order size (as it frequently does). If the unit cost varies significantly, then the formula has to be run at each price break and evaluated. JIT attitudes have a major impact on the E.O.Q. In JIT, you would work with reducing the "C" factor and increase the carrying costs "A." This would reduce the E.O.Q.

EOQ $= \text{SQRT} \ (2 \ (CN)/(UI + A))$

where C = cost of processing an order, receiving, and stocking the material (frequently in the $50–$100 range); N = yearly usage of the part; U = unit cost of the part; I = rate of interest (sometimes called the opportunity cost; could be the prime lending rate 6–12% that banks charge their best customers—some formulas for E.O.Q. add in a factor to "I" for the cost of a stockout); and A = annual carrying cost in the store room, usually in the 10–20% range. For example, our part has an annual usage of $(12 \cdot 52) = 624$ units per year. The unit cost is $10.00. We will use $100 to process the order: 10% for interest and 15% carrying cost:

SQRT $(2 \ (100 \cdot 624)/(10 \cdot 0.1) + 0.15)$
          $124,800/1,15 = \text{SQRT} \ 108,521 = 329$ is the E.O.Q.

How to Calculate Turns: Turns evaluate the efficiency of the money invested in the maintenance inventory. When turns equals 1, the inventory value is used up once a year.

Turns $= (P \cdot S)$

where P = annual purchases of parts and spares, and S = stock level in dollars. For example, if your department purchases $1,200,000 each year and the inventory on the shelf equals $600,000, then turns = (1,200,000/ $600,000) = 2.

Cost of the Maintenance Inventory

Cost of Money: Your organization could invest the money now tied up in inventory at market rates and get a secure yield from 5% to 10% in today's market. Some organizations use a factor called "opportunity costs" which could be significantly higher than borrowing rates.

Expenses of Warehousing: This includes depreciation on building space and shelves, an allocation of utilities, building maintenance and security, life cycle costs on material handling equipment, forms and paper, office supplies, and machinery. Cost is usually figured at 2.5% to 6.5%.

Taxes and Insurance: Some localities tax the assets of the organization; most have real estate taxes—this also includes casualty insurance or reserves for self-insurance. Costs vary from 1% to 3%.

People Costs: Full-time stock clerks, allocation of other clerks, pick-up/delivery people, supervisors. Overall parts volume has a great influence, and the cost is from 10% to 40%. Large or very efficient stock rooms could run ratios lower than 10%.

Deterioration, Shrinkage, Obsolescence, Cost of Returns: Parts sometimes become unusable, disappear, are obsolete, or must be returned for warranty or incur a restocking fee. Costs vary from 4% to 15% (higher if shrinkage is a significant problem).

Saving Money by Reducing Inventory on the Shelf

Big Ticket Analysis: Most of the dollars on your shelf are tied up in relatively few big ticket items. These $500–$5000 and up parts represent over 50% (and as much as 80%) of the dollars invested. Steps to free up money and space start with making a list of all of your big ticket items. Look at the list and ask four questions of each part.

1. Does this item belong in the inventory at all? Has the unit it was purchased for been retired?

2. Is the item a special insurance policy item (long leadtime part for a critical machine)?

3. How many should we really stock?

4. Is there an alternate strategy for handling this, such as vendor stocking, consignment stock, group stocking (one plant holding the part for several potential users), reengineering to eliminate need, or taking the risk of not having the part and waiting for it?

To reduce your inventory, look at the answers to these four questions. In most inventories, 10%–20% of the dollars can be eliminated without impacting the ability to respond to maintenance demands.

Traffic

The mission of traffic is to move freight into and out of the plant by the most economic method, consistent with the delivery timing requirements (see Fig. 23 for an example). Traffic saves the organization money by knowing the best modes, carriers, and strategies for moving freight. Maintenance usually represents a minor headache to the traffic department. The typical maintenance shipments are LTL (less than truckload) and time sensitive. Modes of shipment include truck, rail, air, other. Within each mode there are several distinctions.

Truck can include small package delivery, LTL, truckload, special trailers (drop frame, flatbed, refrigerated). Truck also includes permitted loads (too large, heavy or dangerous for conventional moves). Rail cars have similar characteristics but have almost double

Traffic Decision: Best way to ship parts from Chicago to Birmingham

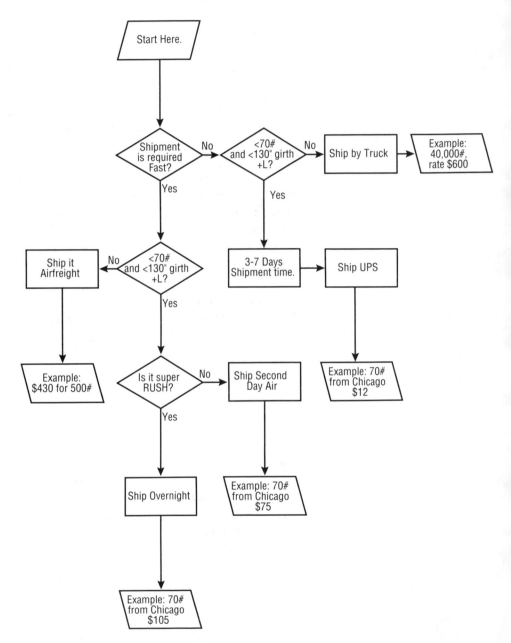

Fig. 23.   Traffic decision matrix.

the size and weight of trucks. Types of rail cars include boxcars, tank, flat, and special cars.

Air freight includes small package delivery service, regular air freight, regular airlines airport to airport, charter. Occasionally helicopters are used to deliver freight to places that are hard to reach. Other shipment modes include all special moves including barge, ship, courier, and anything not already mentioned.

Costs within each mode are determined by weight, distance, and class of commodity. For example, one of the lowest cost commodity classes is Class #50—iron and steel fittings. The reasons Class 50 is inexpensive to move by truck are that the products are hard to damage, are dense (small cube with high weight), and are not usually desirable for theft. A high-cost commodity class would be computers, which are easy to damage and are low density (the trailer would be full before weight limits are exceeded). Theft exposure is also high. The following terms are used in shipments.

FOB (City, Shipping Point or Delivered): This means Free On Board (scller will load truck or rail car). The FOB point is important because of both the responsibility for the shipment and the freight charges. FOB delivered keeps the vendor responsible for the shipment until it reaches your door. FOB shipping point or FOB originating city makes you responsible for the shipment. If an FOB Philadelphia shipment is damaged, you still have to pay for it and then submit a claim with the carrier.

FAS: Free Along Side (you are responsible for the loading charge) is commonly used for ships or very large freight.

For most maintenance departments, the preferred method is UPS Ground on small shipments. If more speed is needed, then go to Federal Express or UPS Second Day, then Federal Express Priority or UPS Red Label. Large shipments are to be handled by other air freight companies such as Emery, DHL, etc.

10.

How to Manage Maintenance with a CMMS

Computerized Maintenance Management System (CMMS)

The reason we computerize is the same reason we manage maintenance in the first place. We computerize to lower or avoid costs, improve service, control costs, ensure uptime, improve quality, etc. We also computerize because running manually looks bad in the eyes of our peers and ourselves (called the "because factor" by Jay Butler in *Maintenance Management*).

Some high-tech firms computerize for the last reason because maintenance is the final department of the organization that is still done manually. It is sobering to see the maintenance managers of some august high-tech organizations explain that they cannot get PC's and software to help their effort. This reinforces the belief that maintenance is a very low priority and cannot get attention or resources for improvement.

Many maintenance departments are grappling with the decision to computerize. It is actually a surface decision for a much deeper decision. A decision to computerize is also a decision to treat maintenance as a serious profession. The decision to computerize is also a decision to impose discipline on a group of mechanics (who are traditionally very independent and hard to control). The computer is a tool that maintenance managers imagine will allow them to predict, affect, analyze, and eventually control what goes on in maintenance. This computerization decision and the deeper decisions that it represents go to the core of the culture of maintenance in your facility.

The reason that most CMMS installations go astray and never realize their promise is because the inquiry that the system came out of was not wide enough. In other words, the firms thought they were only computerizing, and so they only asked questions about hardware, software, and databases. They never asked themselves the deeper questions: what are we about? how do we view maintenance? what is our role for the next several business cycles?

In the old model of maintenance, mechanics are looked at as fixers/maintainers, not as thinkers. It is logical in the old model to assume that the tradespeople have no reason to interface with the computer, and that additional people are needed to enter the work orders and other data.

Maintenance leadership time is clogged up with paperwork, cracking the whip, quality inspections, meetings, and the problems of scarce resources. They are already working long hours just to keep the ship afloat. There is no time to even read a report, let alone deeply study an issue. Using other resources is a joke because the maintenance engineers, planners, and analysts are mostly gone due to cutbacks or are buried in regulatory/safety issues, and endless meetings.

Herein is the dilemma of the computerization effort. How we grapple with this problem will, in large part, regulate how well the system is used. There is only one solution to this problem in the new paradigm of maintenance management, and the solution is distasteful for many organizations. The solution is as follows.

- Mechanics and tradespeople will enter their own data. We should help them in all ways possible—with bar code scanning, rational data structures, and streamlined data entry.

- Mechanics and tradespeople will know how to (and are encouraged to) analyze data to uncover and solve problems. We should help them by standardizing types of analysis and teaching predesigned models.

This view threatens the status quo. Even more than that, it threatens the way we look at our mechanics. Our mechanics have far more mental capabilities than we give them credit for.

We never forget that computerization of maintenance is a complex job when measured against other computerization efforts. The first reason it is so complex is due to the nature of the data collected. Maintenance data have copious detail and flow in a variety of channels.

Data: Who called in, time called in, time complete, elapsed downtime, what they reported, why do the repair, where the event came from, who authorized it, what priority, where to deliver the parts, when was the last time this happened, what to service, parts used, supplies, trade, technician, hours, crews, bench time, rebuild effort, crafts, assets, components, subcomponents worked on, what was done, downtime, what the mechanic saw or recommends, who to charge, comments from the mechanic, comments from the operator, what cost center, etc.

Channels: Telephone, E-mail, face to face, fax, computer networks, engineering drawings, specifications, gauges, MAP systems, PLC networks, cycle counters, store room communication, time clocks, authorizations, locations, machine tags, old history cards, written communication from mechanic/from operator, verbal communication from mechanic/from operator, evidence from the broken parts, outside laboratories, etc.

The second reason that computerization of maintenance is so difficult is that maintenance information systems are among the most complicated packages commonly found in industry. To compound the problem, knowledge about good maintenance practices is not well distributed throughout the organization.

People from accounting, data processing, or even production do not have enough expertise in maintenance to be of much help in choosing software. On the other hand, the maintenance department people are usually not knowledgeable about the other business systems to which maintenance must interface.

Maintenance is low priority when it comes to attention from data processing. Work on maintenance systems is not usually viewed as mission critical. This leads to a common situation where the maintenance system is delayed years, and eventually the maintenance department bootlegs a small stand-alone system that does not talk to the organization's other systems. Data being generated by the maintenance system are not available to other departments, and the decisions they make reflect this ignorance.

Most organizations focus on picking the right system vendor and the right package. Successful implementations of computerization also focus on the readiness of the organization to accept the new computerized culture. This new culture needs to be sold to all parties involved and interested in maintenance. Without adequate preparation, the system—at best—will only enjoy a superficial acceptance. To improve acceptance, the training effort must start well before the system is selected.

Selecting and installing maintenance software is a major effort that will require the time and energy of key maintenance players. The best implementations have the support of the mechanics, supervisors, and other maintenance staffers before the system is turned on. To facilitate this, involve as many levels of the maintenance department as practical in the search for a system.

After choosing a system—with the guidance of the vendor and both the maintenance and data processing management teams—encourage the supervisors and lead mechanics to do the research and help type in the system's masterfiles. Kent Edwards, Vice President for Four Rivers Software Systems (the organization that markets the TMS package), has a rule of thumb that no more than 90% of the system setup should be done by either the vendor or the customer. That ensures the expertise of the two groups is commingled. For a more complete discussion, see the section on setting up your PM system. This includes a detailed discussion of the steps necessary to set up the CMMS.

Before you decide on a system, answer the following questions.

1. Is there enough time, money, and interest to involve all levels within the maintenance department and other stakeholders in the decision process to buy CMMS? Is there support from top management to see you through the inevitable ups and downs of the entire installation process? Management support is essential.

2. Sufficient resources for a complete installation are also essential. The resources include training dollars, time replaced on the shop floor, and computer access. If necessary, can you get typing and basic computer skills training for your mechanics? Will management tolerate the initial research and keying of files by your mechanics and staffers? Can you get the budget

authorization to replace the mechanic's slot on the shop floor by overtime or by a contract worker?

3. After the maintenance system is in operation, will mechanics and supervisors have the training, knowledge, positive attitude, and access into the CMMS to investigate a problem? Is there continuing training in advanced concepts beyond "which key strokes to get which reports"-type classes? Is there regular time set aside for thinking and using the system for research into problem areas? Do mechanics and supervisors have easy access to terminals or PC's? Are these devices hardened against the shop environment?

4. Is there organizational willpower to ensure that garbage and faked data will be kept out of the system? In other words, is falsifying a work order to fill 8 hours viewed as a joke or a crime? Will the data coming out of the system be commonly held by management and the workers to be accurate and useful? Are maintenance records treated as seriously as payroll or other accounting records?

5. Does anyone (including mechanics) have the time to investigate repair history to detect repeat repairs, trends, and new problems? Related to question 3 above, do they have the training to use the system to answer the questions that they have?

6. Can you and your staff spend enough time designing the system's categories to make meaningful comparisons between like machines, buildings, and cost centers? This is a two-step process. The first step is to have the vendor's trainer conduct a class in the category model of that system and how things are commonly handled. The second step is to actually fight out the categories that you want to use. It is critical to understand and wrestle with the decisions that you make at the early steps in the setup of a system.

7. If you have 100 pumps, probably 20 of them create the most maintenance load. This rule of management has tremendous application in maintenance. It is called the Pareto principle. Has the Pareto principle (the 80/20 rule) been taught and

used to isolate the "bad actors" (that is, to identify the problem machines, craftspeople, or parts)? Be sure you understand how to generate the Pareto analysis or exception reports in the system you chose.

8. Will you have the support of a responsive data processing department (or a very responsive vendor)? You will want changes, fixes, enhancements. In fact, your ability to handle technology and sophisticated systems will improve after the first 6 months. Many organizations outgrow their first systems in a year or two.

9. Does the longer range plan include CMMS integration with stores, MRP, purchasing, payroll, CAD/engineering? The trend is toward company-wide networks. Organizations want everyone discussing a problem to be working from the same data. This means linkages of the maintenance information system to the corporate information systems with all the links and hooks that that implies. Increasingly, information systems are viewed as strategic advantages. Access to information makes a major difference.

How to Look at and Compare Systems

Shopping for a system is a daunting undertaking. There are 200 or more vendors of software for maintenance. There are an additional 250 vendors in specialized areas such as fleet maintenance, building maintenance, etc. The salespeople learn that no sale takes place unless someone in your organization gets excited about their offering. To create excitement, the salesperson shows you how to solve real problems with the inquiries and reports from their system. You complain about a PM problem—they show you the PM screen that solves the problem. You would like to track the costs going into a machine you are building—they show you cost accumulation reports. There is a problem for you with this approach.

The reason that systems fail in their implementation rarely has to do with the lack of reports or inability to get information out, but rather from a basic misfit between the system and the existing maintenance culture or organizational requirements. If your culture requires mechanics to keep log books, and the system you chose doesn't support that format, then they might rebel against the duplicated effort. If you use a 16-digit asset number for accounting purposes, then the 10-digit field will not do. These pitfalls can be avoided by looking at any prospective system using a technique described in the next section. Look at the parts of all of the prospective systems in the same sequence.

Discussion of the Maintenance Management Application

All business applications (software packages), maintenance management included, have four logical components. Together these sections are the "system." The completeness and quality of the system depends on the care, knowledge, and goals of the designers of the system in the four areas. When you are choosing a system, designing a new system, or revamping an older system, consider these components separately. A maintenance system might consist of several to more than 500 programs. All of the programs are linked together to form what you see as a seamless system.

Part 1—Daily Transactions: This includes all data entry such as work order, packing slips/receipts of parts, payroll information, energy logs, and physical inventory information. A defect in this section of the package is usually fatal. It is usually very difficult to repair or reprogram this section for the vendor. The main reason that problems here are fatal is the amount of time your staff will spend facing these screens. The second reason is that defects here will adversely impact all other parts of the system and may limit the usefulness of the system.

Look for: Completeness, quick data entry, logical format, consistent format, and alternate data entry paths. Alternate data entry paths include work order, log sheet, standing work order, string PM entry screens. The more flexible, the better. You will spend more time entering data into a maintenance system than anything else. Most of the garbage that will plague you will enter at this point. Data elements not collected at this point tend to become problems later. For example, a coal-to-coke manufacturer did not collect the data element "who performed the work," as a result, they could not look at rework or callbacks to determine who needed additional training.

Also look for consistency. If three people enter the same repair differently (and the system allows that), the computer will have limited ability to analyze that data. An example would be: #1 Replaced bearing A2, #2 Thrust bearing on shaft 'A'-R & R, #3 I unscrewed the housing D1 put my hands around the end of the shaft holder and . . . These could all be the same repair. A person rather than the computer would have to decide if they were the same.

The other aspect of consistency is system editing. Better systems test data coming in against the masterfiles or with logic to determine that it is valid. For example, equipment ID numbers are checked to see if they are valid (already in the file), subsystems are checked to see if they exist for that asset, etc. Some systems will not allow you to log a repair that isn't on the master repair list for that asset, such as changing the tires of a pump. Other checks might be that you can't close a work order before you open it, or that meter readings go up unless the meter was replaced.

A good system might go through 50 different edits to keep false data out of the database. Total vigilance is required to keep them out of your database. Garbage in your database undermines all of your work. One of the rules of data processing is to move the data entry chore as close to the generator of data as possible. Any firm that decides to go that way should be aware that their training bill will be high for the first year since 20 people (or more) will have to be trained.

Lack of speed is the greatest killer of systems. Clumsy data entry design will cause a revolt among the mechanics or supervisors (whoever enters the information) and lack of compliance with the system requirements. To test speed of a system, develop a set of 4–5 typical work orders. Enter them into the target systems and count the keystrokes or time the process. This would give you one way to evaluate competitive systems. Be careful that you are making a fair comparison between like levels of detail capture. A fast system might fail because it doesn't collect enough details. Indications of a speedy design include on-line look-up tables to ease the way when the work order is missing data, copy function for common repairs, speed typing where you can type the first few letters and have the computer fill in the rest, field duplication keys and programmable defaults (with the most common choices as defaults). The other thing to look for are speed keys (such as Alt + Function keys) to move around the system to avoid the slow but friendly menu structure.

Some of the alternate paths for data entry include bar code scanning, modem or LAN communications from other data systems (such as time card information from the time keeping system), direct feeds from MAP (manufacturing automation protocol) systems such as downtime records, and radio transmission from hand-held terminals. Verbal data entry is starting to show up in selected venues.

Part 2—Masterfiles: The masterfiles are the fixed information about the assets, parts, mechanics, and organization. The masterfile structure reflects the designer's biases more powerfully than any other part of the system.

Look for: Completeness is the big issue because it is very difficult to add any fields to a masterfile after it is in use. Not having space in a masterfile for information that you want to store (perhaps after system is in use) is a common major difficulty. If a data element is not in a master file and it is not collected in data entry, then it is not in the computer. If it is not in the computer, then you cannot analyze it with the computer. The easiest example of this problem is when you want to look at maintenance activity related to some outside facts such as downtime, shift change, or even contract negotiation. If those outside data items are not on the computer, then all analysis will be manual.

In large networks or mainframe computers, the data might be in another system. In that case, the analysis could be done with special programming on the computer or in a spreadsheet package. The usual process to determine the contents of the major masterfiles is a two-step process.

The first step is to look at your data needs. Make a list of the elements necessary to produce the information you need to manage the operation. The second step is to survey several systems' masterfile layouts to look for good ideas and additions. (The first step could be repeated after the system survey.)

One system—TMS—has 105 64-character fields in the equipment masterfile. The first 10 fields are reserved by the system for their canned reports and inquiries. You have 95 large fields to store information. Systems such as TMS are very flexible. The price you pay for flexibility is that the setup is more complex and requires more effort. You have to design the system! On another system there was a field of 35,000 characters (that's about 8 pages of information) for comments!

Typical Data Required for the Asset Masterfile
(Typical record for a water pumping system. Information is taken off a Mechanical Asset Information Sheet)

Asset number:	MWI #4
Asset description:	Water pump system
Location:	South basement main building
Manager responsible:	V. Santiago
Manufacturer:	Pacific Pumping Company, Oakland, CA
Model number:	Series III
S/N:	51B39721
Specs, Elect.:	3 pump units tied together through control panel 208V, p, 178 amps max.
Connection to which asset:	Cistern, process water system, electrical system panel #4
Condition:	One of the three pumps is broken and is out of service, the other two alternate weekly
Work to be done:	Rebuild or replace bad unit
Estimate:	Central pump quoted $12,000 to rebuild.
Prob. of replacement:	Immediate on 1 unit, 5–10 years on other two.

(From Asset Detail Sheet)

Vendor:	Universal Plumbing Contractors
Installer:	Universal Plumbing Contractors
Date installed:	1972
Date in service:	1973
Original cost:	Unknown (part of general contract not detailed)
Warranty:	1 year
Control panel	Pacific Pump
Model	Series III

In better systems, there is a masterfile with all report headings, utilization fields (hours and pieces are never mixed), and screen headings (possibly called a heading master). The advantage is that you can adjust the language of the system to your present language and culture.

Part 3—Processing: The daily transactions are processed either in a traditional batch mode or online. Processing updates the PM schedule, summarizes detailed repair data for reports and machine histories, and keeps all financial accounts current.

Look for: Does it work? Process some data through the full cycle and see if all the accounts, schedules, and masterfiles are updated correctly. Accuracy and completeness are the difficult areas in this item. Most of your bugs will occur during unusual processing conditions.

Reset the system's clock for the year 2000 and run some work orders. Print some reports that include 1990's data with 2000 data. Many bugs will show up in software that uses the last 2 digits of the year (instead of all 4 digits) to calculate elapsed time. Test if possible by printing a report on a machine. Then add a work order on that machine. The test is to print a second report on the machine, which should be different from the first by exactly the amount of the work order that you entered.

On a mainframe system, the processing program represented 4 or 5 months of intensive work. After the original programmer left the company, none of the other programmers wanted to venture into the code. Instead, they insisted on fixing the problems by rewriting the entire sequence from scratch.

Part 4—Demands, Reports, Inquiry Screens: The demands on a maintenance system include reports and screens. There should be reports when there is a large amount of data or when analysis is required. Inquiries should not have to require going to print. Imagine how you expect to use the system and then see how the system will behave.

Look for: Seek many different ways to look at the data, complete basic set of reports and screens, future ability to alter or add reports/inquiries to suit your changing needs and growing expertise.

The reports and screens are the reason that you bought the system. You've been feeding data and maintaining masterfiles for this payoff. The reports should be useful, not too detailed (with the ability to go to a detail level), include the information you need (not results from 10 other divisions), and should be easy to read.

An example of useful levels of detail can be taken from the popular financial program Quicken® (by Intuit Corp.). You can ask for a summary of the totals of all money spent by category. If you highlight one total and double click the mouse, the detailed transactions that make up that number pop up in a window. Hitting the Escape key returns you to the original report. In this way, the details don't overwhelm you and are easily available.

A Canadian maintenance manager complained that his system gave him too much data. Every week he was treated to a 1400-page report of all maintenance information with detailed comparisons to other divisions. He referred to three or four pages and occasionally skimmed the report to see what his buddies were doing in his old division. This is a waste of resources and paper. He asked to have a weekly summary and a monthly or quarterly "big" report. Information services reported that they couldn't find the time to make the change.

The following three types of reporting are commonly available.

Batch Level/Listings/Rehashing of Masterfiles: This is a structured listing of information already in the files. Reports of this kind might include a listing of all assets in the finishing depart-

ment with date of purchase. These reports are frequently required to answer corporate questions about assets, employees,
or other fixed information. They can save hours over manual
techniques. For the computer software vendors, these are the
easiest programs to write, and they assign the lowest paid programmers to the project.

*Comparisons, Performance, Analysis of Database in Relation-
ship to Standards:* This type of report is very useful for benchmarking a maintenance operation. Measures such as maintenance
hours per manufactured unit (man hours per automobile assembled or per ton of steel rolled), maintenance dollars to parts
dollars, percent overtime, or percent emergency hours can re-
veal the actual condition of a maintenance department. This type
of reporting usually flows up to management in the summaries
of benchmarks for the whole operation. In a shop running under
the new paradigm, these benchmark numbers are made available
and discussed with all maintenance personnel.

*Exception Reporting, Division of Reports Exceeding Upper and
Lower Parameters:* When you have specific questions about
problem areas or opportunities for savings, you use the parame-
ter-driven reports from this group. You might think that the new
equipment in the mold shop is breaking down more than the
older equipment. An exception report comparing the two
groups would give you the answer. Powerful maintenance systems have industry standard query languages (such as SQL) to
allow all sorts of ad hoc reporting when questions come up. The
newest systems do not require the services of a programmer for
these reports (you design the report as needed).

Computerphobia: The Fear of Computers

As you begin to use computers in your maintenance operation,
you may run into resistance. Some of the resistance might be due to
fear of computers. After conducting seminars with psychotherapists
on computerphobia, we have come up with some ideas about this
widespread condition.

1. Some fear of computers is normal for people who don't come in regular contact with them.

2. There are degrees of computerphobia from mild anxiety (very common) to full panic attacks (rare). The more mild forms can be dealt with successfully, with a little understanding, in most job settings.

3. The antidote for the fear is systematic contact. Plan to gradually introduce the phobic person to the computer system, increasing the amount of contact over time. Basic to this technique is to support them, especially early in the process.
   A. In the early stages, pick well-defined tasks.
   B. The tasks should be chosen so that success is assured.
   C. Training and computer time should be kept short in the beginning and gradually increased.
   D. Tasks should gradually get more complex along with training.

In our experience, once the initial fear is worked through, computerphobiacs become the system's greatest boosters.

Getting Started in Computers

- Take a positive approach to computers, and become computer literate. Acquire a personal understanding of the fundamentals of computers.

- Get a computer at home. Talk to friends (or your kids) who work with computers (they are usually looking for people they can introduce to computers).

- Talk to/visit similar operations that are computerized. Identify computer users similar to yourself in terms of type, size, and geographic area. Find out what they are doing with computers, how they obtained their computer programs, what computer programs they use most, what makes and models of computers they are using, and whether they are satisfied.

- Know the specifics of your business. Begin to list things you expect from your computer. When you visit trade shows for your industry, collect all of the computer literature and talk to the salespeople. Look closely at the screens and reports. Ask questions if there is anything you don't understand.

- There are inexpensive educational opportunities all around you. Courses are given by local high schools (night programs), technical schools, community colleges, and computer stores.

- Join a local user group for your computer type. Call a local college and ask the computer department for the address of the local user group (or for a student who is a member). If you have an IBM or PC clone, contact the national user group PC-SIG.

Fifty Questions to Help Your CMMS Search

In order to avoid the most common pitfalls of choosing, purchasing, and installing computer control and information systems, ask yourself—and ask vendors—questions about the system. (Both the Maintenance Fitness Questionnaire and the section on installing PM systems have additional ideas.) A full-function CMMS should be able to help your operation in many areas. Many organizations purchase systems to solve specific problems; they don't need other functions or don't consider them important at the time of purchase. The following 50 items will help you focus your attention in various areas. They are not in priority order.

Work Order

1. Produce an easy-to-use work order that allows future conversion to bar codes, hand-held terminals, and other technological advances.

2. Classify all work by some kind of repair reason code: PM, corrective, breakdown, management decision, etc.

3. It should be easy for a single person to screen work orders entered before authorization for work to begin. Some systems have a field that has to be checked by a supervisor or manager to release the job to the next processing step.

4. Print an up-to-date lock-out procedure on all work orders automatically. It will have the ability to access a lock-out file and incorporate the right lock-out scheme (there might be only 10 variations for the whole plant). Less desirable, but still OK, would be an individual lock-out file for each machine.

5. Automatically cost work orders. Look up the value of a part in the inventory and bring the cost across to the maintenance work order. Also look up the charge rate for the individual mechanic.

6. Provide status of all outstanding work orders. Allow sorts on different status codes. An example would be to print or display all work orders waiting for engineering.

7. Record service calls (who, what, time stamp, where, how), which can be printed in a log format.

8. Allow production to find out what happened (what status) to their work request without being able to make changes.

9. Calculate backlog of work and display it by craft.

10. Both open and closed work orders can be displayed or printed very easily. Keep work orders available for at least 5 years, and preferably from birth to retirement of the equipment.

11. Facilitate labor scheduling with labor standards by task, ability to sort and resort the open work orders by location of work, craft, and other ways.

Stock Room

12. Facilitate big ticket analysis by printing all parts over $500. Facilitate A–F analysis by printing the product of (in descending order) the unit cost times the annual usage.

13. Store room part of the system has part location to help the mechanic or store keeper find infrequently used parts.

14. Generate a parts catalog by type of part or by current vendor, with yearly usage to facilitate blanket contract negotiation.

15. Recommend stock levels, order points, order quantities.

Maintenance History and Reporting

16. Maintain maintenance history that is detailed enough to tell what happened years later.

17. Provide information to track the service request—maintenance work order issue—work complete—customer satisfied cycle. Include elapsed time and other analysis factors.

18. Provide reports for budgets, staffing analysis, program evaluation, performance.

19. Provide information for work planning, scheduling, and job assignment. Has the capability to store and retrieve work plans, copy old work plans, and modify existing plans when new information comes in.

20. Be able to isolate all work done (sort, arrange, analyze, select, or list) by work order, mechanic, asset, building, process, product, division, floor, room, type of equipment or asset.

21. Provide the ability to easily structure ad hoc (on the spur of the moment) reports to answer questions that come up. This is called a report writer.

22. Has the ability to generate equipment/asset history from birth (installation, construction, or connection) to present with all major repairs and summaries of smaller repairs.

23. System reports are designed around Pareto principles, where the system helps identify the few important factors and helps you manage the important few versus the trivial many.

24. System reports on contractor versus in-house work. System can track contractor work in as much detail as in-house work.

25. Provide reports charging back maintenance cost to department or cost center.

26. Has reports with mean time between failures (MTBF) that show how often the unit has failed, how many days (or machine hours) lapsed between failures, and the duration of each repair (MTTR).

27. Highlight repeat repairs when a technician needs some help.

PM System

28. Allow mechanics to easily write up deficiencies found on PM inspection tours. System then automatically generates and tracks a planned maintenance work order.

29. Automatically produces PM work orders on the right day, right meter reading, etc. PM system can sort work orders by location to minimize travel time.

30. Be able to display PM work load for a future period, such as a year by week or month by trade.

31. Be able to record short repairs done by PM mechanic in addition to the PM and actual time spent.

32. Support multiple levels of PM on the same asset (such as a 30-day A-level and a 180-day B-level on the same asset); reset the clock if the high level is done (if you do a yearly rebuild, the monthly PM clock gets reset). A resetting feature prevents a 30-day PM coming up a week after a rebuild.

33. PM's are generated by location by trade to facilitate efficient use of people and minimize travel.

34. Allows the input of data from predictive maintenance subsystems. This might include trending, days to alarm, baselining, comparison to previous readings.

35. Highlights situations where the PM activity is more expensive than the breakdown.

36. Has simple reports that relate the PM hours/material to the corrective hours/materials to the emergency hours/materials. This will show the effectiveness of the PM program. These ratios become benchmarks for improvement.

General

37. System can handle 3–4 times more assets than you imagine ever having. Even medium-sized and smaller companies go on acquisition hunts. A small successful manufacturer might find itself tripling (or more) in size overnight.

38. System has a logical location system to locate assets and where work is done.

39. System tracks the warranty for components, and flags warranty work to recover funds.

40. Easy to use and learn for novices, and quick to use for power users.

41. System is integrated or can be integrated to purchasing, engineering, payroll/accounting.

42. System easily handles a string PM such as a lube route, filter change route.

43. System runs on standard computer hardware (not special hardware incompatible with everything else). The system is compatible with existing Local Area Networks (if it is a PC product).

44. System vendor has the financial strength to complete the contract (and stay in business for several years after installation).

45. The vendor has software support people whom you can easily reach, via an 800 number. Once you get through, the people know the product and maintenance of factories.

46. The vendor provides economical customization. They have ongoing enhancement. The programmers are employees of the vendor or contract workers.

47. The vendor has a local installation organization.

48. The vendor is experienced in management of installation projects of the size of your facility; they have start-up experience with projects this size.

49. The vendor's technical people are well cross trained (software, hardware, and reality wear, like how a real machine works). It's important that the installation people have experience with maintenance.

50. The vendor has been in business 5 years or more.

11.

Managing Maintenance Through Planning, Scheduling, and Project Management Techniques

There is some confusion about the difference between the functions of scheduling and the functions of planning. Part of the problem is that the two functions are frequently compressed together, particularly on smaller jobs. The easiest way to differentiate between scheduling and planning is to think of a military battle. Military planners look at several probable scopes of the battle, predict the duration of the engagement and the number of troops needed, then decide on the best equipment needed and calculate the logistical support for the troops and weapons. The military planner will also look at the command and control issues (battlefield communications and supervision). The plans developed might be put on the shelf as a package awaiting a "go" from the commanders.

The plan is independent of execution. Nothing has been ordered, deployed, or moved in the real world. The maintenance plan is the same as the battle plan. It lists all of the resources needed, approvals, material/part/supply lists, tooling requirements, access requirements, time, skills, and any special information or requirements.

In the military, getting a "go" from the commanders begins the execution phase of the plan. Troops, ships, ordnance, aircraft, support units, logistical units, and intelligence are scheduled into a the-

ater of operations. Food and supplies are ordered. Spare parts and
reserve troops are put in place. Orders might be placed for parts,
ordnance, fuel, and food to fill up the pipeline emptied by what
should be used. The battle plan is revised based on changes from
intelligence gathered. It is turned over to battlefield managers. Fundamentally, the success of the battle depends on the quality of the
initial plan. While many a battle was saved by individual valor and
genius, no one would argue that the right plan makes it easier.

The same things are true in the maintenance world. A bad plan
might be saved by individual heroism or genius, and it's still easier
to work from even an adequate plan. When we are ready to start
the maintenance job (the battle), we would say that in this phase
the planning is over and the scheduling, coordinating, and management phases begin.

Maintenance Planning

On larger jobs, you can save 3–5 hours of execution time for
every hour of advanced planning. Advanced planning is a proactive
skill. The pressure is on doing the job, not planning the job. Few
users scream at you to plan repair jobs. This section shows the steps
for successful maintenance planning. The plan consists of a detailed
list of the work to be done and an evaluation of each of the five
elements of a successful maintenance job. The work to be done is
the first part of the planning process. The goal of the plan is to
enumerate all of the resources needed for a job to avoid all of the
avoidable collisions of these resources.

Some resources showed the average ratio of planners to mechanics in various crafts in heavy industry.[1]

Electricians	1:20
Welders	1:11
Machinists	1:14
Riggers	1:24
Pipefitters	1:17
Laborers	1:30

[1] *Maintenance Management,* by Jay Butler, published by University Seminar
Center (address in the Resource section).

Very few organizations now have full planning staffs. When organizations still have planners, the job has been expanded to include computer "feeding," permits/safety duties, and other staff functions. These numbers might be a guide as to the amount of time that should be spent planning by the people in the craft themselves. In addition to the normal time the mechanic spends doing routine planning, the chart shows an additional 5% of high-level planning for electricians, 7% for machinists, and almost 6% for pipefitters. Use these as guides if your tradespeople are expected to plan their own jobs.

Questions to be Answered Before Proceeding:

What job is to be done?

What is the scope of work?

What is the priority of this job?

What are the work steps?

What is the likely elapsed time? (Plans must be considered about the probability that the job is significantly larger than first thought.)

Is engineering required? (If engineering is required, order drawings and specifications.)

Once the scope of the job is complete, then details have to be ironed out about each of the five elements.

Mechanic(s), Techs, Helper: What skills, how much craft coordination, time per step, crew size, contractor needed, back-up plan if the scope of work isn't adequate and job doubles or triples in size.

Tools: What tools, where to procure, how to ensure availability, vendor for rental or purchase.

Materials/Parts/Supplies: What parts, how many, availability, in stock, lead time, vendor.

Availability of the Unit to be Serviced: Best time to do, check production schedule for likely times. Look for the best time in the business cycle for a window to repair an item. Determine the effect of this repair on related units.

Authorizations/Permits/Statutory Permissions: Hot permit, open line permit, tank entry, lock-out/tag-out, EPA involvement, Safety Department.

What Does Planning Do?

- Maintains packages on all jobs planned but not started.

- Inspects job and discusses the scope of work priority with customer.

- Looks into history files to see if this or a similar job was done.

- Determines the scope of the job. Makes sketches if necessary.

- Breaks job into smaller projects or job steps.

- Prepares work order. Gets authorization if it exceeded authority.

- Writes out work plan (steps to complete project).

- Locates all materials in stores.

- Determines lead times and vendors for nonstock materials.

- Determines special tools and equipment needed for job.

- If asked, plans longer term requirements such as yearly PM requirements by month.

The planner (or the planning function) is a key to the effective daily operation of the maintenance department. Competent planning requires a wide range of skills.

Qualifications for Planning

- Ability to think of jobs as having both mechanical aspects and abstract (time, tools, space requirement) aspects.

- Ability to communicate well, both verbally and in writing.

- Gets along with others.

- Can work with different types of people from all levels in the organization.

- Can represent the organization's interests in discussions with outside firms.

- Has knowledge and skills in one or more crafts.

- Is interested in crafts other than those with which they are familiar.

- Has respect of craft workers.

- Has a positive attitude toward company, supervisors, and managers.

- Has the ability to plan work and foresee problems (doesn't like surprises).

- Understands or can be taught job planning and scheduling.

- Computer literacy (or can be taught; has positive attitude).

- Some training in budgeting.

- Understands the issues of the user department.

Scheduling

1. A schedule brings together, in precise timing, the five elements of a successful maintenance job: the mechanic(s), the tools, the materials/parts/supplies, the availability of the unit to be serviced, and the authorizations/permits/statutory permissions.

2. In order to bring the whole job under control, you control the parts. You must manage at the time and at the level where you can have a useful impact. Review the work plan to see if the situation has changed in any material way. An accurate plan is necessary to know where and when to manage the individual job steps.

3. The key is monitoring the whole operation—repair by repair, mechanic by mechanic, and day by day. Monitoring means keeping ahead of jobs that are going to start, and checking in on jobs in process. Materials and parts are common culprits that can cause a well-planned job to go awry. Parts require constant attention and chasing, scrounging, persuading, pleading, and sometimes yelling.

4. If a large repair is falling behind schedule, supervision is notified within a short time so that the situation can be corrected while they can still have an impact on that job. Waiting until a monthly meeting to find out that a job went overtime is too late.

5. Work should be quantified in the job plan. A reasonable amount of work is expected each day. Workers are freed from a hurried atmosphere one day, and a "kill-time" atmosphere the next.

6. Management's expectation as to how much work is a reasonable day's work is given to the mechanic in advance. Intermediate goals are identified and checked by the supervisor.

7. An inevitable byproduct of this approach is the uncovering of many hidden operations problems. Planning highlights areas where mechanics cannot do their job due to a problem outside their control, and other problems with the old way of doing business. These previously hidden (or unpublicized) problems suddenly come into the foreground, as in the following situations.

   • Mechanics being pulled off to work on nonproductive activities is a common problem—i.e., the maintenance department is also used in personal service to the plant higher-ups. Mechanics running to the airport, picking up contracts, or setting up for picnics cannot adhere to a work plan or stay on schedule.

   • The planning package is horrendous if it does not reflect reality. Parts are wrong, job steps are outdated or wrong, lock-outs and new regulations are not included.

- Stock room contributes to schedule-miss conditions regularly. Items shown on the inventory are not on the shelf. Quantities are wrong. Stockouts are frequent on regularly used items. Excessive time is spent waiting for clerks.

- Failure to put equipment back into service when promised builds the attitude in production that they never want to give up a machine because they never get it back when promised. This attitude stands in the way of communications, and contributes to the problem of inability to get control of production equipment when scheduled.

- Lack of cross training causes clashes of resources. You might have enough maintenance people, but are in chronic short supply of computer or instrumentation skills. The cause is lack of flexibility because of single-skilled tradespeople. There are some good arguments for craft shops. We have to face the fact that a craft shop is less productive and adds an additional potential collision (enough people, not enough of a critical craft) to reduce productivity.

How to Set Up a Schedule

1. Identify and assign unique names/codes to all crews, teams, or individuals.

2. Design a priority system that will help determine what should go first when you don't have enough people.

3. Physically build a scheduling board (or two); you can use 4' x 8' of plywood. List the crews, people, or teams across the top. Build slots so that each crew or individual can have their work orders visible, in order of priority.

4. Review all jobs in backlog and add priority.

5. Load (slide work orders into slots) jobs starting with highest priority. Choose a crew for the repair. If you experience frequent emergencies, leave a percentage (equal to your historical emergency hours) of your crew's time unscheduled. Alternatively, leave certain crew members off the schedule for hot jobs when you start up.

6. The schedule should be updated every day to visually reflect the actual status of all jobs. Red flags can be used when jobs fall behind. When the mechanics pick up jobs, they should leave a copy or other indicator that the job is pending.

7. If you build two scheduling boards, fill the second one with jobs due in the next period. When it starts, the board will be up-to-date and ready to go. If you are running on one board, keep removing completed jobs and start to load future jobs below.

8. The twice-each-shift checks are to be coordinated with shift changes and meal breaks, and all jobs should be evaluated for status relative to the schedule. Jobs which the schedule showed as complete should be complete. Milestones should be met on longer jobs. Shorter jobs that spanned a check should be informally reviewed.

9. Followup with supervisors and management should take place when reviewing job progress.

Jobs of the Scheduler

Job Tracking:

• Secure permits and ensure that safety instructions are in the hands of the craftspeople or their supervisors.

• Maintain a tickler file on all projects that have been started.

• Notify and consult with customers about any pending interruptions or disruptions.

• Update the physical schedule; prepare dispatch sheets in consultation with supervisor.

• Get information about status of all repairs on a regular basis.

• Review all projects for their adherence to the plan.

• Be alert to continuing schedule-miss conditions. Detect when a job runs into trouble before it misses a milestone.

- Secure special tools and equipment as defined by the plan before the job is to start.

- Attend weekly meetings to discuss work progress, progress on projects, updates on materials.

- Clean up paperwork at the end of the job. Verify that the job was done according to the plan. When a job deviates, learn why. If necessary, update the plan.

- Complete daily, and add to, weekly reports for higher management.

- Be alert to continuing schedule-miss conditions.

- Update the planning package.

Material/Parts/Supplies Tracking:

- Follow up on availability and delivery of parts for planned work orders.

- Call outside vendors (before jobs start) when parts are late in order to get parts that might slow down or stop a scheduled job.

- Get the purchasing department involved when a vendor is being unreasonable or is suspected of lying.

- Verify that material is on hand. Keep a check on most-used and critical items in stores. If appropriate, place parts in a protected area.

- Prepare requisitions for jobs.

- Work on outage to assure more accurate usage information on parts.

- Update the work plan with actual part usage.

Why Scheduling Techniques Work

There are several reasons why scheduling works, and why it improves the quality of life in the organizations which use it in an enlightened way. These reasons are rooted in psychology, and one reason (at least) goes back to the early pioneering Hawthorn studies at the Chicago Hawthorn plant of Western Electric.[2]

The study found (to compress a huge body of work into a few sentences) that workers at Western Electric responded—with increased productivity—to attention from management. The classic study concerned the effect of lighting on productivity. When lighting was increased, productivity went up. When lighting was decreased, productivity again went up. After many experiments, the "attention" factor was found to be critical.

The schedule organizes the attention of management and applies the attention where there is a problem. The attention will naturally cause the productivity to go up, and the higher levels of management can also apply their problem-solving skills to a real problem at hand.

Frequently, the reason that a schedule-miss occurs is related to the mechanic not having a critical piece of information, special tools, techniques, experience, or the necessary material. The supervisor, having been informed, can intervene and get the job back on schedule.

The schedule helps a mediocre supervisor become a good one.

Project Management

On larger jobs, the techniques of project management can be used to control the project. Note that project management was one of the first areas to be implemented on microcomputers, so there is a wide variety of packages in all price ranges.

There are techniques to efficiently manage large repairs. The planner should be conversant in the major ways to set up and manage jobs. In a nutshell, the project management packages require you to list all of the subprojects, resources, and dependencies. From this information, the software builds a model of the project and tracks it in real time, with alerts when you fall behind or when there are resource conflicts.

[2] For a complete account, see Friz Roethlisberger and W. J. Dickson, in *Management and the Worker,* published by Harvard University Press, 1939.

History

We are indebted to Harry L. Gannt of the Frankford Arsenal in Philadelphia for developing a systematic technique for tracking and scheduling projects. Developed in 1917, the Gannt chart is one of the oldest planning tools available to maintenance managers.

Since then, dramatic improvements have been developed to manage larger and more complex projects. The CPM (Critical Path Method) improved the ability to determine the critical events that could hold up a large project. The PERT (Project Evaluation and Review Technique) system, a refinement of CPM—including the ratings most optimistic, most probable, and most pessimistic—was adopted by the military.

One of the first projects where PERT was tested was the design and assembly of the first nuclear submarine (Polaris class) *Nautilus*. The Navy and Electric Boat in Groton, CT, had to schedule 250,000 major activities of 250 contractors and 9000 subcontractors in the multiyear project. At any given time, delay in any one of hundreds of activities could throw the whole project off schedule.

They used the PERT project charting and management method. Because of the complexity of maintaining the critical path—due to the project changing, activities being complete on schedule, ahead of schedule, and behind schedule—the entire system was eventually programmed in FORTRAN and run on the then-powerful IBM 360 mainframe. The project was completed close to schedule and budget.

The Concepts are Extremely Powerful

1. Collisions of labor/material/tooling/machine/order are substantially easier, cheaper, and faster to resolve on paper than in the field. This is also a golden rule of planning.

2. There exists a group of activities within the project, the sum of whose times regulates the length of the project. The longest path through the project (that includes these activities) is called the critical path.

3. We also know that time estimates are more likely to be incorrect by being too short rather than too long. On the Polaris

program, they used a distribution called the Beta distribution, which is not symmetrical. The more pessimistic (overdue) estimate had the greater probability.

4. If you keep the ever-changing critical path on schedule, the project will run on schedule.

5. Conversely, if the critical path falls behind schedule early in the project, you know the whole project is in trouble, and only an intervention (more labor, expedite materials, etc.) can bring the project back on track.

How to Set Up a Gannt Chart[3]

1. List all activities for the project:
   A. An activity has a defined beginning and ending
   B. No other activity can start in the middle of the activity; if one does, then split the one activity into two activities
   C. Determine time for each activity; optionally, determine effort level
   D. You might list three times: optimistic, probable, and pessimistic
   E. Determine what activities must be complete for this activity to start.

2. Using Gannt-type charts, start adding activities and block in the times. Start the activities in the appropriate time block.

3. On the first planning pass, use relative time (elapsed days, weeks from day one). When the actual beginning date is known, redo the chart to absolute (date) time.

4. Be alert to conflicts in labor/materials/tooling/machine/safety/permits/order. If you optionally added effort level, then you can sum the columns by craft to determine number of people required for the project.

[3] Much of the information on the Gannt, CPM, and PERT charting methods was taken from *Production and Inventory Control,* by Plossl and Wight, published by Prentice-Hall in 1967, and from the *1990 Scheduling Guide for Program Managers,* by Defence Systems Management College.

5. All of the activities along the longest path are critical path activities. Slippage in any critical path activity will result in the project being late.

6. There is a certain point at which, if delayed, noncritical path activities become critical.

7. After the project is started, mark off the projects that are completed. Estimate the durations of the uncompleted projects and shift them on the chart. Recalculate the critical path. If anything is out of bounds, then plan your intervention.

12.

Maintenance Quality Improvement

Quality control is hard to define in maintenance. The usual definition in production is that quality means to consistently produce parts with low variation. Maintenance quality usually deals with the effects, not the repair itself. In some circumstances, maintenance quality might mean reduced downtime. In others, it might mean reduced scrap, faster startup, quicker response, no repeat repairs, keeping unit in spec, no interruptions, or a satisfied user.

Every maintenance operation should define quality in a way that is useful to their operating environment. The late W. E. Deming was considered the quality "guru" for the last generation of Japanese quality experts. In fact, the quality award in Japan today is called the Deming award. He had much to say about quality in manufacturing. The surprise is that Deming's points apply to maintenance also. We just have to see what quality is in our plant, site, or division.

W. E. Deming's Fourteen Points

The following points were first discussed in 1950! (See the section on the 20 Steps to World Class Maintenance in Chapter 1 for additional discussion.)

1. Create constancy of purpose toward improvement of product and services with the aim to stay competitive, stay in business, and provide stable employment. Maintenance deterioration usually takes a long time. Any effective maintenance strategy must also have a long horizon. Resources

must be allocated for good maintenance practice, and not taken away with every bump in the quarterly results.

2. Adopt the new philosophy. Awaken to the challenge. Take responsibility for (and leadership in) change. Our maintenance departments often are the last areas of the organization to realize the need for change. The department is dragged kicking and screaming into the new corporate culture. Looking toward the future, I see a maintenance department providing leadership for the rest of the organization. Nowhere else is high quality so closely related to safety and to high self-esteem. Quality is intertwined with the very history and culture of the crafts.

3. Cease dependence on inspection to achieve quality—build quality in. Quality comes from skilled and knowledgeable mechanics given good tools, adequate materials, and enough time to do the job. Quality comes from choosing well-designed equipment that doesn't need much maintenance. What maintenance the equipment does need is easy to perform and get to. Quality comes from pride in a job well done. Lead by example, with ceaseless training, coaching, and systems analysis. When defects occur, concentrate on the system that delivered the defect rather than having a preoccupation with finger-pointing.

4. End the practice of awarding business on the basis of price alone. Instead, minimize total cost. Move toward a single source for each item, and toward a long-term relationship of loyalty and trust. A revolution in purchasing is at hand. More and more organizations are looking at the total costs of a part or the life cycle cost of a machine. Some economies are false and hurt the overall goals of the organization. A low-cost bearing might be the most expensive bearing you ever buy.

5. Improve constantly and forever the system of production and service, to improve quality and productivity, and thus constantly reduce costs. In today's market, the way it used to be done is never going to be good enough for the future. All improvements and growth flow from dissatisfaction with

the status quo. Build measurement into the maintenance information system. Continually strive to improve both the visible and the invisible performance.

6. Institute training on the job. Training should be mandatory for mechanics the way it is for doctors or teachers. Our factories and facilities have today's levels of technology, but our maintenance people have yesterday's skill sets. To maintain effectiveness, we must train to bridge the gap. Special attention should be given to the people on your staff who deliver the on-the-job training. These informal trainers need instruction in how to teach adults. They also need backup materials to deliver the best possible training.

7. Institute leadership. The aim of supervision should be to help people and machines do a better job. The supervisor should serve the subordinates by removing the impediments from production. The supervisor should ensure that the mechanic, the tools, the parts, and the unit to be serviced converge. The supervisor should also be the lightning rod for disruptions from management and production (unless there is an emergency, the mechanic should not be disturbed because interruptions reduce quality and worker satisfaction).

8. Drive out fear, so everyone may work effectively for the company. Fear of the loss of a job interferes with the mechanic's ability to concentrate. Fear gets in the way of the pride a mechanic feels in a job well done. A flexible and highly productive department where people can shift from trade to trade—maintenance to construction to production—is the safest one.

9. Break down the barriers between departments. Everyone's expertise is needed for constant improvement. With scarce resources, we must include knowledge from other departments and groups to come up with the best overall solution for the organization. Maintenance problems can get complex quickly, with financial, marketing, purchasing, quality, and engineering ramifications. The best solution to a problem might not be the best maintenance solution (e.g., run until destruction to fill an important order). Information for

the best solution might come from another department and another area of expertise.

10. Eliminate slogans, exhortations, and targets asking for zero defects and new levels of production. Such exhortations create adversary relationships. The bulk of the problem for quality and production belongs to the system, not the people. Stable processes create quality. Create stable processes, producing quality outputs, and people will want to achieve the objectives without cohersion and alienation.

11. Eliminate work standards, quotas, and management by objectives (MBO). Work standards and quotas are associated with management styles that treat the maintenance worker like someone who needs to be told exactly what to do and how long to take. Standards are useful for scheduling and to communicate management's expectations. It is difficult to not use them as a production whip. That is a disaster in maintenance situations because we want the mechanic to take the time needed to fix everything they see (within reason!), not just the original job. We must trust the mechanic to look out for our interests particularly when we are not there. The problem with MBO is that it focuses on visible, measurable aspects of maintenance. Many of the real issues of maintenance concern aspects of the environment that are hard to measure.

12. Remove the barriers that rob the worker/engineer of his/her right of pride of workmanship. The responsibility of supervisors must be shifted from numbers to quality and improvement. Tradespeople must be allowed to feel pride in jobs that are well done. Maintenance managers and supervisors must not allow anything to stand in the way of that pride.

13. Institute a vigorous program of education and self-improvement. World class maintenance departments make a commitment to invest 1–3% of their hours in training for all maintenance workers. Technologies are changing, so skills must change, too. A world class auto manufacturer mandates 96 hours of training per year for everyone. A high-tech manufacturer requires 110 hours.

14. Put everyone in the organization to work to accomplish the transformation. This transformation is everyone's job. This transformation requires the talents of all the employees—all of the talents of each person. When a hotel chain had the housekeepers meet with the architects (for a new hotel), the result was concrete suggestions to improve the designs that reduced maintenance costs and improved the rooms for the customers.

Obstacles to Success

1. Lack of constancy of purpose when planning a product/service which will have a market and keep a company in business (and provide jobs). Maintenance issues (like the wearing out and failure of a compressor or boiler) take a long time to develop. Only an equally long-term view will be effective. A changing agenda for the goals of maintenance works against the department.

2. The supposition that solving problems, automation, gadgets, and new machinery will transform industry. Maintenance problems are people problems. The systems, attitudes, and approaches are at issue. The view of maintenance as a necessary evil—or of maintenance workers as grease monkeys— must be transformed. The transformation starts in the minds and hearts of the maintenance department and then flows to the rest of the organization.

3. Emphasis on short-term profit, short-term thinking fed by fear of unfriendly takeover, and by a pressure from bankers and owners for dividends. Top management will squeeze maintenance to reduce costs below the level that is necessary to avoid deterioration. The cost reduction is temporary, the asset will deteriorate, and long-term integrity of the process will be compromised. Maintenance requires long-term planning and commitment.

4. Evaluation of performance, merit rating, or annual review. The purpose of annual reviews and performance rating should be that something *useful* results. In most cases, the

quality and quantity of output of a mechanic is more a function of management interference than operator qualities. Annual reviews rarely change behavior.

5. Transience of managers and job hopping. For one beverage bottler, the average tenure of the maintenance manager was 22 months; some lasted as few as 9 months. All came with bright ideas and wanted to prove themselves. The result was a complete lack of focus on long-term goals and plans. As each manager tried to cut costs, the negative results fell to the next player. This job hopping in management without a master plan dramatically exacerbates the short-term view.

6. Management by use of only visible figures, with little or no consideration of figures that are unknown or unknowable. For example, when you invest in training for your maintenance crew, where does the increased asset show up? When, after spending hundreds of thousands of dollars in a long, expensive trial-and-error development process, a firm finally develops expertise in a new process. This expertise (this new asset) is nowhere on the balance sheet. It is important to measure and also to realize that much of what goes on in maintenance is unknowable.

7. Expecting instant success. Changing a fundamental process takes time. In the current U.S. culture, it is hard to imagine instituting a change in process that could take 5 to 6 years. In actuality, if you start with a typical reactive maintenance department, it could take you 5 years or more to create a proactive TPM-type partnership in maintenance and production.

8. Following other examples. We think that if something worked in another machine shop or foundry, it will work in ours. Since maintenance in factories has no strict rules, examples from our industry may not be useful or even relevant.

9. "Our problems are different." Actually many people's problems are the same. In the PM area, while no two plants will have the same exact schedule, the problems will be the same. In our public sessions, maintenance managers in in-

dustries of very different size and sophistication marvel at the similarity of the problems.

10. Poor teaching of statistical methods in industry. Industry is just waking up to the value of statistical methods of explaining what happens in the shop. Application of simple statistics to PM or PCR intervals would improve effectiveness. Simple relationships such as failure to PM's would show the effectiveness of the frequency you have chosen. Statistics replaces seat-of-pants reasoning, panic logic, and historical prejudices with testable and verifiable conclusions.

11. "Our trouble lies entirely within the work force." Your production system is a stable system to produce a certain number of defects. Changes in the work force are irrelevant to the output. Only changes to the system can have an impact.

12. False starts with *inadequate* planning, top-level support, and follow-through kill quality improvement transformation in most places. Serious thought and planning are needed before starting. Commitment must start at the highest levels in the organization. Buy-in at each level must be earned, worked for, and appreciated before proceeding to the next level.

13. "We installed quality control." The quality control is a way of life; it is a staple. You don't install it, you become it.

14. The unmanned computer is one of the dangers of wholesale computerization of maintenance. The computer is a great tool that (like any great tool) is frequently misapplied. Allow the people to have their say and make sure the computer answers to someone (a real person) who can overrule the machine.

15. The supposition that it is only necessary to meet specifications. Many of the important aspects of a component are not included in the specifications. You never know which attributes are important until you try changing vendors, and find out that your entire process depends on qualities of a particular vendor's products that are not covered by the specifications.

16. The fallacy of zero defects. Every system produces defects. Ultrahigh quality requires enormous sample universes to establish the defect rate.

17. Inadequate testing of prototypes. By starting manufacturing on inadequately tested prototypes, we strain the system of improvements. There will be so much ground to cover before everything stabilizes that the product will be half-baked for a long time. To leapfrog this phase, exhaustive testing should be built in.

18. "Anyone that comes to try to help us must understand all about our business." The sad truth is that if the solution to your problem was commonly known in your industry, you would probably know what to do.

Techniques for Continuous Improvement in Maintenance

Without continuous improvement in the delivery of maintenance, there is stagnation and complacency. What seems like a secure situation gives way to an eventual upheaval when management realizes that maintenance is not keeping pace. What is at stake could be the survival of your organization (if not of your department or job). There are competitors that are eyeing your market share and they are not standing still.

There are opportunities in every maintenance operation. An internal study done by a major maintenance provider in Canada estimates the opportunity as follows.

Percentage of Possible Savings of Maintenance Budget Dollars

39%	Reengineering and maintenance improvements
26%	PM improvement and correct application of PM
27%	More extensive application of predictive maintenance
7%	Improvements in the store room

Let's first agree on what continuous improvement means in the maintenance department's context. The standard narrow definition would just concern reductions to the maintenance labor, parts, and contract work. The wider definition includes other cost areas where maintenance has a major impact. Continuous improvement means *either* ongoing reductions in: labor (operator, mechanic, and contract); management effort (reduce headaches, nonstandard conditions requiring management inputs); maintenance parts/materials; raw materials; energy; machine time; capital; and overhead; or improve reliability (uptime) and repeatability of process (quality), and improve safety for the employees, the public, and the environment.

Continuous improvement is a five-step process. The steps are commitment, measurement, information gathering, investigation, and then action. In the sections that follow, we will look into each area.

Commitment

Organizations that are committed to continuous improvement commit the time to do the analysis necessary. These organizations have established that appropriate effort in continuous improvement provides a substantial return on investment. They allow and encourage maintenance workers to participate on problem-solving teams that involve other departments of the organization, including production, engineering, quality, cost accounting, and marketing. Effective commitment also is a long-term choice. In good and bad times, the maintenance department must always be looking at improvements.

Measurement

A necessary prerequisite to continuous improvement is establishing ways of measurement of the maintenance department. Without measurement it is difficult to determine if an operation is truly improving. The process of setting up measures is called "benchmarking." There are three types of benchmarks used by maintenance departments.

1. *Internal* benchmarks are based on prior periods in that division. An internal benchmark might be downtime hours due

to maintenance problems. This benchmark would be tracked monthly (or even weekly) or a long period of time. Continuous improvement could then easily be measured against prior periods.

2. *Best-in-class* is a benchmark of the best in your industry. Some large organizations will take the best plant of a certain type (if they have many plants that are the same). Other organizations will review trade literature or initiate a study to determine the best plant in the business and compare themselves to that plant. A benchmark might be the number and severity of customer complaints per month. Compare yourself to the best plant of your type in the industry. Continuous improvement would measure your progress to catch up to them and eventually surpass them.

3. *Best-in-the-world* is the ultimate comparison between functions. A best-in-the-world benchmark might evaluate your telephone answering function and compare it against the best in the world (such as Federal Express or Lands' End). The comparison organization might well be in a vastly different type of business (or even in government or education). Continuous improvement puts your organization against the best there is. Your achievements against the best-in-the-world's benchmark are tracked and reported upon.

Information

To achieve this goal, examine all production data, all minor jam-ups, all failures, all short repairs, all PM activity, and all other maintenance events for opportunities to reduce the inputs or help the improvements.

Experimental Model: Shewhart Cycle (see Fig. 24)

1. What is the most important accomplishment of this team: what changes? what data? plan tests? how to use data?

2. Carry out the test or change on a small scale.

3. Observe effects of change.

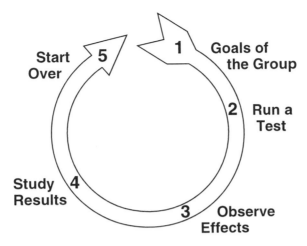

Fig. 24.   Shewhart cycle.

4. Study the results: what did we learn, what can we now predict?

5. Start over with knowledge accumulated.

Investigation

Review the production and then the maintenance incident history (an incident could be a breakdown, a series of breakdowns, PM's for a machine, a series of minor adjustments, or other maintenance activity). Review the asset, area, or system from six different points of view.

1. Economic Analysis
   A. What is the cost of the incidents?
   B. What is the cost of the downtime?
   C. What is the cost per year?
   D. What is the return on investment of a projected improvement?
   E. How much should we spend to fix this?
   F. What is our investment in this asset or process?

2. Maintenance Analysis
   A. How disruptive is this breakdown?

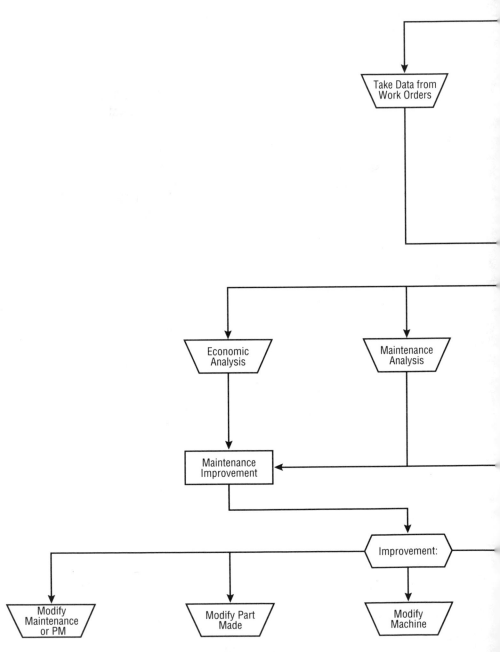

Fig. 25.   Continuous improvement.

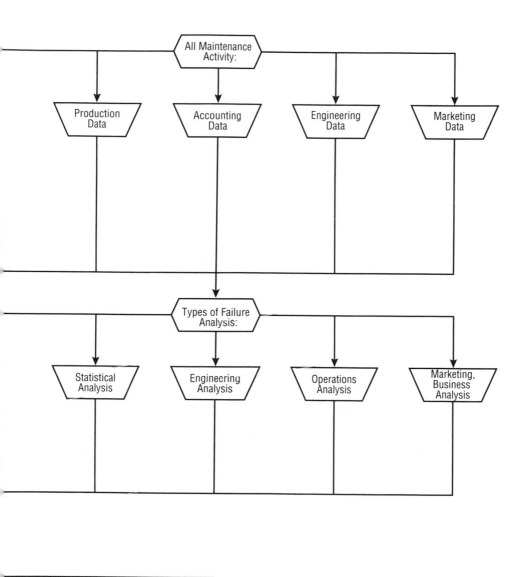

All Maintenance
Activity:

Production
Data

Accounting
Data

Engineering
Data

Marketing
Data

Types of Failure
Analysis:

Statistical
Analysis

Engineering
Analysis

Operations
Analysis

Marketing,
Business
Analysis

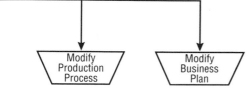

Modify
Production
Process

Modify
Business
Plan

    B. Does this breakdown cause mechanical or electrical problems elsewhere?

    C. What is the honest opinion of the maintenance "old timer" experts?

    D. Is the root cause a faulty or inadequate maintenance procedure?

    E. Is the root cause related to inadequate training in any maintenance skill?

3. Statistical Analysis
   A. How often does the incident occur?
   B. Is there a pattern or trend?
   C. What is the mean time between failures (MTBF)?
   D. What is the mean time to repair (MTTR)?
   E. Can the MTBF be managed by replacing the component more frequently than the failure frequency (PCR)?

4. Engineering Analysis
   A. What was the mode of the failure?
   B. Is a structural analysis of the broken parts indicated?
   C. What happened just before the failure?
   D. Why did the breakdown take place?
   E. Was there a failure of the PM system?
   F. Do the PM task lists look at this failure mode?
   G. Are we looking at the root cause or a symptom?
   H. Is the root cause related to an inadequate part specification?

5. Operations Analysis
   A. How does this event impact operations?
   B. Does the event force the failure of other parts of the process?
   C. Can we bypass the problem with a backup or standby unit?
   D. Is there a scrap or start-up exposure?
   E. Is this indicative of a failure of the operations system?
   F. Is inadequate operator training a cause or a contributor?

6. Marketing/Business Analysis
   A. What is the impact of this failure on the customer (internal/external)?

B. Can we afford to have this type of event happen?

C. Can this event impact quality?

D. Does this impact morale?

E. Is there an impact outside our sphere of influence (environmental, competition)?

F. How high should the priority be to deal with this problem?

G. Is there a regulatory or legal impact to this event?

H. Is there a logical business decision indicated (outsourcing the part, sell off product)?

You can see from the scope of list above that no matter how knowledgeable individual maintenance professionals are, they cannot know all of the ramifications of a major maintenance event. If continuous improvement is seriously pursued, multidepartmental teams will be necessary on an ad hoc basis to attack problems.

Action

Based on the investigation, institute improvements in one or more of five areas.

1. *Modify maintenance or PM procedure.* Add tasks to catch the particular failure mode earlier on the critical wear curve. Increase the technology of the tasks, such as adding a shock pulse meter or vibration analysis. Increase frequency of the tasks. If economic and business analysis shows that we are spending too much on PM in relationship to other costs, do the opposite of the above (reduce frequency, depth, etc.). Investigate better cleaning, improved lubes, better alignment processes (if this is a wear problem). Design easier-to-do maintenance procedures and reengineer the equipment to suit.

2. *Modify machine (maintenance improvement).* Improve the machine so that it doesn't break or need adjustment. Improve the tooling. Make it easier and faster to do the maintenance tasks. Automate some of the maintenance tasks. Remove the source of the problem (redirect the dirt so it doesn't fall on

the cylinder). Add automated lubrication systems. Add instrumentation to the machine.

3. *Modify part/product.* Make the part easier to produce. Improve the tooling. Change the shape, size, material, finish. Reduce (or increase) the number of steps. Reduce (or increase) the part's specifications. Simplify the steps. Job out the part.

4. *Modify the production process.* Improve the whole process. Improve incoming materials. Improve the process to allow greater variation in incoming materials. Make the transfers more bullet-proof. Look for improved technology. Look for a whole new and more reliable process. Give headache processes to vendors who are expert in that process.

5. *Modify the business or marketing plan.* Discard the product, increase the leadtime, buy your competitor, sell out to your competitor, raise prices, sell custom units, have your competitor make your parts/you make theirs, hire a top engineer/ production person or consultant to help smooth the process.

Continuous improvement is the only antidote to the constant pressure of competition. It is essential that management realize that continuous improvement in the maintenance department is everyone's business and can only be achieved with everyone's input. The goal of continuous improvement is the elimination of the need for maintenance. The inputs drop and drop until maintenance is nonexistent. While you can't expect this outcome soon, the goal is there to work toward.

Reliability Centered Maintenance (RCM)

One of the best models for continuous improvement is the application of reliability centered maintenance. RCM is one of the most powerful ways to improve maintenance because it addresses the core of the customer need, that is, an increasingly reliable system. The technology is an outgrowth of investigations into reliability on behalf of the airline industry.

RCM is a five-step process. The process is usually team driven with members from both operations and maintenance. It is facilitated by an RCM specialist with good knowledge of the process.

1. *Identify all of the functions of the asset.* At first, this might seem trivial. On a second examination, there are many secondary functions that are important. Functions are divided into primary, secondary, and protective. Each function is defined by a specification or performance standards. For example, the primary function of a conveyer is to move stone from the primary crusher to the secondary crusher. The specification calls for 750 tons per hour capacity. Secondary functions include containment of the crushed stone (you don't want pieces falling through the conveyor and hurting someone).

2. *Look at all ways the asset can lose functionality.* These are called functional failures. One function can have several functional failure modes. A complete functional failure would be that the unit cannot move any stone to the secondary crusher. A second failure would be that it can move some amount less than the specification of 750 tons per hour. A third functional failure is that if the conveyor starts moving more than 750 tons per hour, it starts to overfill the secondary crusher. Each secondary function also has losses of functionality. In our example, the conveyor could allow stones to fall to the ground, creating a safety hazard.

3. *Review each loss of function and determine all of the failure modes that could cause the loss.* In our example, the list might be 20 or more failure modes to describe the first functional failure alone. Failure modes of our rock conveyor include motor failure, belt failure, pulley failure, etc. Each functional failure is looked at, and the failure modes are defined.

Use some judgment to include all failure modes regarded as probable by the team. All failures that have happened in the past (in this or similar installations) would be included as well as other probable occurrences. Take particular care to include failure modes where there would be loss of life or limb or environmental damage.

It is essential that the team identify the root cause of the failure and not the resultant cause. A motor might fail from a progressive loosening of the base bolts which strains the bearing causing failure. This would be listed as motor failure due to base bolts loosening up.

It is important to include failure modes beyond the normal wear and tear. Operator abuse, sabotage, inadequate lubrication, and improper maintenance procedure (reassembly after service) would be considered.

4. *What are the consequences of each failure mode?* Consequences fall into four categories: safety, environmental damage, operational, and nonoperational. A single failure mode might have consequences in several areas at the same time. John Moubray, in his significant book *Reliability-Centered Maintenance,* says "Failure prevention has more to do with avoiding the consequences of failure than it has to do with preventing the failures themselves." [1]

The consequences of each failure determine the intensity with which we pursue the next step. If the consequences include loss of life, it is imperative that the failure mode be eliminated, reduced to improbability, or designed out of the system.

A conveyor belt failure would have multiple consequences which would include safety and operational. A failed belt could dump stone through the conveyor superstructure, hurting everyone underneath. The failed belt would also shut down the secondary crusher unless there is a backup feed route.

The failure of the drive motor on the conveyor will cause operational consequences. Operational consequences have costs to repair the failure itself as well as the cost of downtime and eventual shutdown of the downstream crushers. Other failures might only have nonoperational consequences. Nonoperational consequences include only the costs to repair the breakdown.

[1] *Reliability-Centered Maintenance,* by John Moubray, published by Industrial Press (address in the Resource section). This is one of the leading texts by one of the leading thinkers in this area. He and his firm Aladon are responsible for much fine work in RCM.

5. The final step is to find a task which is technically possible and for which it makes sense to detect the condition before failure (or otherwise avoid the consequences). If no task can be found, and there are safety or environmental consequences, then a redesign is demanded.

For example, if it is found that the belts start to fail after they are worn to 50% of their diameter, an inspection might be indicated. If the belts fail rapidly after cuts or other damage, then a sensor might catch these problems. In all cases, where safety or environmental damage is the main concern, the task is to lower the probability of failure to a very low level.

We also have to understand that some failures of sensors or protective devices are hidden. A failure is said to be hidden if it occurs and the operators would, under normal conditions, not notice the problem. For example, if a belt thickness gauge fails, then (unless the design is failsafe) the operators would have no way of knowing that the sensor is out of service. Without the protective device, a second failure (of the belt) could occur and cause an accident.

In operational failure modes (such as the motor failing), the cost of the task over the long haul has to be lower than the cost of the repair and the downtime. If the PM task costs $1000 a year and a breakdown costs $2500 and downtime costs $4000 per repair, then the breakdown has a natural occurrence of more often than every 6.5 years. If the failure naturally occurs every decade, then it is cheaper (and smarter) to run in bust'n'fix mode (it breaks and you fix it).

13.

Time Management
in the Maintenance
Pressure Cooker

Preliminary Self-Test: Time Management[1]

1. Are you satisfied with the way you spend your time?   yes no

2. Are you satisfied with the number of hours you work?   yes no

3. Do you enjoy your work?   yes no

4. Do you feel good about the quality of your work?   yes no

5. Do you effectively cope with the stress/pressure of your job?   yes no

6. Do you have enough free time to pursue hobbies and/or community activities?   yes no

7. Do you have time to enjoy your family?   yes no

8. Are you satisfied with the results you achieve?   yes no

9. Are you satisfied with your supervisor's concern for time management?   yes no

10. Are you satisfied with your subordinate's concern for time management?   yes no

11. Does your use of time reflect your goals?   yes no

12. Are you satisfied with the quality of time with your subordinates?   yes no

13. Are you an effective delegator?   yes no

---

[1] Adapted from the National Seminars course entitled "How to Get More Done." (The address of National Seminars is in the Resources section.)

14. Do you react to changes in a constructive   yes   no
    manner?
15. Are you in control of your telephone?   yes   no
16. Do you take advantage of time windfalls?   yes   no
17. Are you well organized?   yes   no
18. Do you have a well-designed plan of organiza-   yes   no
    tion for your desk?
19. Do you take time to exercise?   yes   no
20. Do you occasionally do nothing?   yes   no

Score 1 point for each yes, 0 points for each no.

Score range:
18–20: You could (and probably should) teach time management
    courses in your spare time.
15–17: You are a good time manager.
12–14: You're above average in time management.
9–11: Pay close attention to this chapter!
0–8: You have a lot of work to do. Is your head still above water?

Maintenance can be a pressure cooker. Emergencies, short staffing, vendor problems, and high customer expectations all contribute to a stressful job. While removing the stressors is impossible, changing your attitude might be possible. A person who feels mastery over his/her environment transforms the "bad" stress into good excitement.

Time management helps people feel mastery. The goal is not to feel in control—that would be an illusion. The goal of time management is to feel that you can master anything that comes at you.

Effective time management is a four-pronged approach to gaining control of your day, while multiplying your output. It includes the following activities.

1. Evaluate and shift how you think about time.

2. Complete the four "projects" that show you new ways to work and to think about your time.

3. Practice the seven daily habits of successful supervisors.

4. Use the twenty strategies for dealing with time killers.

The Nature of Time—How Do *You* Spend It?

Time is the only truly nonrenewable resource; unlike energy, it cannot be saved or created. Everyone has the same amount of time—a leader of a multibillion dollar organization has exactly the same number of seconds and hours in the year (31,557,600 and 8766, respectively) as you do. Regarding amount of *time*, we are all truly equal.

TIME MANAGEMENT   =   SELF-DISCIPLINE.

Time management is a life skill—one which managers should hone and sharpen throughout their entire lives. However high you rise in your organization, time management will make you more effective. Good time managers also have time (and sometimes, more importantly, energy) for the other fun things in life like family, hobbies, and contributing to their community.

Do you know how you actually spend your day? Using the form shown in Fig. 26, take a minute to write down the percentage of time you spend at each activity in an average week. Please try to note what you actually do rather than what you'd like to be doing (or what you'd like others to think you're doing). As you consider the percentages, ask yourself whether you are the kind of supervisor you'd like to be. If you're not, ask what that supervisor would be spending his/her time on. In the second part of the exercise, fill in these "ideal" times using the right column.

Use the log sheet shown in Fig. 27 to keep a record of what you actually do for a week. Time management experts agree that you start managing your time when you find out what you actually spend your time doing. Copy the log sheets for as many days as you plan to log. The sheet should be filled out as the day progresses (*not at the end of the day*).

Other Strategies for Finding Out How You Spend Your Time

One of the most effective methods to track activity is work sampling. The key to work sampling is to randomly note your own activ-

Activity	Actual Percent	Best Manager
Budgeting	_____	_____
Circulating (moving through your domain, ensuring work is done and done correctly)	_____	_____
Dealing with users/customers	_____	_____
Engineering jobs	_____	_____
EPA/hazardous waste activities	_____	_____
Failure analysis, other deep thought	_____	_____
Giving job assignments	_____	_____
Inspecting work	_____	_____
Looking for information, drawings, etc.	_____	_____
Meetings	_____	_____
Other regulatory activities	_____	_____
Quality circles, other group efforts	_____	_____
Purchasing/parts-related activities	_____	_____
Paperwork (all other)	_____	_____
Personal activities (all non-company activities on company time)	_____	_____
Reading junk mail	_____	_____
Scheduling, planning	_____	_____
Seeing salespeople	_____	_____
Teaching, training	_____	_____
"Wrench turning" time (all physical work activities)	_____	_____
Other _____	_____	_____
Total	**100%**	

Fig. 26.   Daily activities exercise.

Daily Log   Date___/___/___   Name _____

Time	Activity	Notes
7:00	_____	
:30	_____	
8:00	_____	
:30	_____	
9:00	_____	
:30	_____	
10:00	_____	
:30	_____	
11:00	_____	
:30	_____	
12:00	_____	
:30	_____	
1:00	_____	
:30	_____	
2:00	_____	
:30	_____	
3:00	_____	
:30	_____	
4:00	_____	
:30	_____	
5:00	_____	
:30	_____	
6:00	_____	
:30	_____	
7:00	_____	
:30	_____	

Fig. 27.   Daily log.

ity throughout the day. Each time, note the activity at the instant of the random time. Conway Quality, a firm in Nashua, NH, has developed an entire productivity improvement program designed around a random time beeper. This beeper will beep randomly throughout the day. On specially designed pads, you record your activity. (Their address can be found in the Resources section.)

Reality of Being a Maintenance Supervisor

The reality of the field of maintenance is that frequently we are not in control of our time. *Please note:* when we are not in control of most of our time, it is doubly important to control what little time is left.

The Four Projects

Project #1—Clean Your Desk and Organize Your Office

A. Set aside a block of time when you won't be interrupted.

B. Get an entire box of manila folders. Put them in order, with the tabs alternating left–center–right–left–center–right, etc.

C. Get a blank piece of paper (full sized) for your master "to-do" list.

D. Put all of your papers in a pile. Include the scraps of paper—half/quarter sheets, envelopes, napkins—and everything else you were going to get to.

E. Go through every piece of paper and be ruthless about throwing away as much as possible. Separate into a new pile the papers you need to keep. If there is an action that needs to be taken, save the paper in this new pile.

(Now rest for a few minutes. All of your old piles have been consolidated into a new, smaller pile. In fact, maybe half of your old stuff is now in your trash can.)

F. Back to work. Start with the top paper and ask yourself some simple questions:

    1. Is there any work that must be done? Add that assignment to your master to-do list.

    2. Should I keep the piece of paper? Remember you recorded the assignment. If it's a keeper and no file already exists, prepare a manila folder.

    3. Keep this up until you reach the bottom of the pile. Do not do the work now unless it can be handled within 1–2 minutes.

G. Remove all office supplies such as tape, staplers, all paper clip collections from the surface of your desk. Attack any surface of your office that accumulates papers for more than a very short time (the paper turns over in 1 shift).

H. Apply the same standard to your files and drawers. Review the information and determine if you need the information, and if there is any action that you need to take. Clean your drawers of the debris that accumulates over the years.

You now have a clean desk. You also have a completed to-do list that could be up to several pages long. You will find that a clean desk encourages efficient work habits. You put your work on your desk, complete it to the level possible at that time, put it back into its proper files, and have a clean desk once again.

Project #2—Supercharge Your Time

You have three major tasks: 1) get your immediate job done; 2) have time for the large, important jobs/analysis; and 3) educate yourself to improve your value to your customer.

A. Look at areas where you could do two things at once without sacrificing quality. An example would be the twice-daily commute. An hour commute could translate into over 200 hours a year of learning time through the use of cassettes. Remember that 200 hours is equivalent to 3 college level courses (homework time included). Learn something while waiting for meetings, waiting for airplanes, driving, exercising, taking a bath, mowing the lawn, etc.

B. Carry a microcassette recorder to record ideas, memos, letters, and instructions. This is an excellent idea if you have staff support to transcribe your tapes. The transcription should include a separate page for ideas on each project to be filed in the project file. Your brain is your most powerful tool.

C. Delegate some of your tasks to your crew. A well-trained crew will multiply your effectiveness.

D. Learn to type and use a computer. Once you learn, you will type as fast or faster than you write, with less fatigue and greater accuracy.

E. Use fax machines to transmit ideas (particularly drawings) to remote sites, vendors, and users. It's faster than mail and more accurate than any descriptions.

F. If you drive during the day as part of your job (managing several sites), get a mobile phone. This way, the little ideas that occur to you can be turned directly into action.

G. Learn to speed read. If you think that it is a waste of time, try the following exercise. Time your reading speed. Read this whole paragraph to the bottom of the page fairly closely at your normal reading speed. Note the elapsed time. Divide the total word count (107) by the number of seconds and multiply by 60. A good fast pace is 400 words per minute with good comprehension. Speed readers top out at 1500 to 2000 words per minute. Many maintenance supervisors read at 100 or less words per minute. How much more could you read if you could read at 1000 wpm? Check below.
   (*Note:* Paragraph G has 107 words. A speed reader would have completed it in 6–10 seconds.)

Project #3—The 80/20 Rule

An Italian economist, Vilfredo Pareto, discussed an informal rule now called the Pareto Principle (or the 80/20 rule). It can be

#	MASTER TO-DO LIST	TOPIC	DATE ON	20%/80%

Fig. 28.   80/20 master to-do list.

stated, for most management situations, as the rule that 80% of the action comes from only 20% of the actors. We find that 80% of our employee problems come from 20% of our employees; 80% of our emergencies come from less than 20% of the equipment; 80% of our results will flow from 20% of our activities. If we identify these critical few activities, and increase our time commitment to these activities, we can double or triple our results each day.

Your exercise is to go through your master to-do list (see Fig. 28) and examine each item. Divide the items into a 20% important and highly leveraged activity and the 80% low leverage activity. The 20% activities should be scheduled first during your high energy intervals throughout the day. The top three of these activities become your bottom lines. The bottom line is "if you do nothing else today, you will do your bottom lines."

The low return on investment activities, the 80% activities, will fill in around the 20% activities. For another look at setting priorities, read about the work of Stephen Covey below.

Beware of the tyranny of the *urgent.*
Remember, "You are paid for what you complete,
not what you start."

One of the greatest thinkers and consultants of this era is Dr. Stephen R. Covey. In his excellent books, he describes a new way to sort out events that exactly corresponds to good maintenance practices. His model (reproduced in Fig. 29) describes four kinds of incoming tasks divided up into two categories:

Fig. 29.   The "Urgent/Important" model.

The four types of tasks are: 1) Important—Urgent; 2) Unimportant—Urgent, 3) Important–Not Urgent, 4) Unimportant–Not Urgent.

Type 1: Most maintenance managers are already excellent at this—fire fighting. I've never yet met a maintenance professional that would say they were not great fire fighters. The bad fire fighters probably get winnowed out and go into an allied profession that doesn't have as many crises. You need to be an effective fire fighter to keep your job.

Type 2: This category is the bane of the maintenance professional. Urgency is implicit in most maintenance requests from users. The phone rings and everything sounds important (particularly to the caller). It is tough to separate the important from the unimportant. No one ever got fired from a maintenance job because they responded too quickly to the urgent–unimportant jobs coming into the maintenance center.

Type 3: World class maintenance requires significant attention to events that are important but not urgent. Your whole PM system, your training efforts, and your operator involvement programs fit into this category. No one is usually yelling for you to interrupt production to perform PM's. PM's are essential for reduced breakdowns, but they are not pressing to be complete.

Type 4: This is an easy category. You can see it stacked up on maintenance professionals' desks, on top of file cabinets, in closets. This is stuff you've been meaning to look over but never seem to get time to do. This is usually the fun, brainless stuff like looking through junk mail. It is not really important and definitely not urgent.

The goal of time management for maintenance professionals is to shift time spent from categories 2 and 4 into category 3. Attention to category 3 reduces the category 1 problems in the future.

Project #4—Energy: Establish Your Energy Level by Times of the Day with a Code Such as H (High), M (Medium), L (Low)

	Monday	Tuesday	Wednesday	Thursday	Friday
6:00am	_____	_____	_____	_____	_____
6:30	_____	_____	_____	_____	_____

	Monday	Tuesday	Wednesday	Thursday	Friday
7:00	_____	_____	_____	_____	____
7:30	_____	_____	_____	_____	____
8:00	_____	_____	_____	_____	____
8:30	_____	_____	_____	_____	____
9:00	_____	_____	_____	_____	____
9:30	_____	_____	_____	_____	____
10:00	_____	_____	_____	_____	____
10:30	_____	_____	_____	_____	____
11:00	_____	_____	_____	_____	____
11:30	_____	_____	_____	_____	____
12:00pm	_____	_____	_____	_____	____
12:30	_____	_____	_____	_____	____
1:00	_____	_____	_____	_____	____
1:30	_____	_____	_____	_____	____
2:00	_____	_____	_____	_____	____
2:30	_____	_____	_____	_____	____
3:00	_____	_____	_____	_____	____
3:30	_____	_____	_____	_____	____
4:00	_____	_____	_____	_____	____
4:30	_____	_____	_____	_____	____
5:00	_____	_____	_____	_____	____
5:30	_____	_____	_____	_____	____
6:00	_____	_____	_____	_____	____
6:30	_____	_____	_____	_____	____
7:00	_____	_____	_____	_____	____
7:30	_____	_____	_____	_____	____
8:00	_____	_____	_____	_____	____
8:30	_____	_____	_____	_____	____
9:00	_____	_____	_____	_____	____
9:30	_____	_____	_____	_____	____
10:00	_____	_____	_____	_____	____
10:30	_____	_____	_____	_____	____
11:00	_____	_____	_____	_____	____
11:30	_____	_____	_____	_____	____
12:00am	_____	_____	_____	_____	____
12:30	_____	_____	_____	_____	____
1:00	_____	_____	_____	_____	____

	Monday	Tuesday	Wednesday	Thursday	Friday
1:30	_____	_____	_____	_____	_____
2:00	_____	_____	_____	_____	_____
2:30	_____	_____	_____	_____	_____
3:00	_____	_____	_____	_____	_____
3:30	_____	_____	_____	_____	_____
4:00	_____	_____	_____	_____	_____
4:30	_____	_____	_____	_____	_____
5:00	_____	_____	_____	_____	_____
5:30	_____	_____	_____	_____	_____

Seven Daily Habits[2]

Seven daily habits will help you focus your time and energy so that the important things get done. For most people, identification of the high return on investment activities is difficult. The seven habits institutionalize processes to identify what is important.

These habits help your time management in several ways. They will: help you use your whole mind through utilization of ideas or "aha's;" ensure balance so that you spend time on others and yourself, in addition to work; and give you time for exercise, diet, and rest.

1. There are three activities to help you set up your day—with them, you approach each day with resolve and calm. Without a focus, we become slaves to the urgent and never see the important things. Spend some quiet time and do the following three activities. (Many people schedule this time the night before; others work on this early in the morning.)

   a. *Purpose:* Have a coherent purpose to your work situation (keep this private). Read and review this purpose every day. The purpose should cover what you are moving toward. Some people like to look at this as their personal mission statement. It could include information about your

---

[2] We can thank Robert Allen and his associates at Challenge Systems for combining the work of Napoleon Hill and others with their own ideas to come up with the seven daily habits of success.

purpose at work or at home, information about what you
want for your family, the importance of spirituality in your
life, and how you expect to contribute to the world.

b. *Planning:* Spend a few minutes each morning (or the
night before) planning your day. Consider your purpose
statement. Review your bottom lines and see what elements can be incorporated now. Under the best conditions, your plan may go down the drain, but having a plan
increases the probability that there will be a positive
outcome.

c. *Preview:* Visualize your day as being the way you would
like it to be. Practice in your mind's eye. Many great sports
figures practice in their mind before they swing the club,
bat, or shoot the ball. They *see* success. We need to look
at our work plan and see success in the elements. We see
in our powerful mind the successful meeting with the boss
or a solid coaching session with one of our people.

2. Your first task every day is to schedule and do the thing in
your plan that you "fear" or resist most. Fear stops people
from being outstanding contributors to their organizations,
communities, and families. If, each day, we face one of our
little fears, we would move forward quickly with our agendas.
It is said that anything is achievable if fear can be felt and
then overcome.

3. Schedule and complete the three most important tasks
(called bottom lines) to support your purpose in the following areas: work, others, and self. Complete the "bottom lines"
sheet (shown in Fig. 30) every month. These daily bottom
lines should be met each day, even if nothing else went right.
By doing the bottom lines even on the "bad" days, you move
closer to completing the important (but not urgent) activities.

4. High efficiency depends on a healthy body. Be sure to plan
for adequate rest, good nutrition, and daily exercise.

5. Write down any ideas that come to you about your situation
or life in general (work or home). These insights are called
"aha's." Your brain is more powerful than the biggest computer made and is switched on all of the time. Many insights

This Period's Bottom Lines   Period: _____ to _____

Period Theme: _____

In addition to my normal activity, I will devote high-priority time to building character and balance by improving my life in the following ways.

Family:
1. _____

Being or Brain:
1. _____
2. _____

Body:
1. _____
2. _____

Time or Delegation:
1. _____

People:
1. _____
2. _____

Money or Work:
1. _____
2. _____
3. _____
4. _____

Fig. 30.   Bottom lines.

are outcomes of thought processes that you are not aware of. Noting these insights enriches your life and uses the brain more effectively.

6. Be a teacher or mentor to another person. Every day, one element of your mission is to return something to the people around you. Schedule yourself to be in a position to mentor or coach another person everyday.

7. Review your day—see where you did well and where you would make changes. This is like reviewing films of last night's game. The coach looks at the film with the players with the intention of improving play. A good coach will say what is necessary to improve the players: this includes congratulations, yelling, suggestions, and anything else that would modify behavior.

Bottom Lines

The bottom lines are translated (in pieces) to the individual daily scheduling pages. Each large one is broken into several small ones that can be done in one day. The key is that doing bottom lines advances you toward your goals in the direction of your purpose.

Family: One of your bottom lines is to serve your family in some way. Even if you don't have children, the rest of your family is important for balance. Balance is essential for long-term stability, health, and some level of happiness. An example would be to take your kids to a park once a month.

Being or Brain: Improve yourself. An important bottom line is to invest in yourself. This could be in the form of reading a book, taking a course, or trying something new. An example would be to read one book this quarter on maintenance management. The being also includes your spiritual life—e.g., to pray, attend services, or engage in other religious activity.

Body: Your body is your means to getting things done. Health cannot be guaranteed. You could exercise every day and eat right and still have health problems. Healthy activities can contribute to your quality of life and can help keep you healthy. Items on this bottom line might include to walk at least 30 minutes, 4 times a week.

Time or Delegation: There are many specific ways we could improve our delivery of service. We need to invest some of our time increasing our time effectiveness. This could include training on a new computer program that will make your time more effective. This bottom line could also be to delegate more activity. To delegate, you might have to train a subordinate or seek out a new vendor.

People: Successful people rarely are total loners; they usually have a group of people whom they trust and can go to for advice. This bottom line fixes your attention on this aspect of success. Every month, work to build your "master-mind team."[3]

Money or Work: You may have thought this was all that there was to life. Your company might agree. That's why this entry gets four lines and the others get only one or two!

Descriptions of the Areas on page 1 (Fig. 31) of the Scheduling Sheets

Date: Write today's date in this space.

Day's Theme: Sometimes days seem to have themes. This is optional.

13 Item Scoring: Give yourself 1 point for each of the important items that you can check off. Time in morning or evening is well spent making decisions about the day. You choose your "feared" task, 3 bottom lines, do your review, etc.

Feared: Feared tasks first. Pick an important item that you have been avoiding. This frees you up for other activity. Many people get stuck avoiding their feared task, which blocks other useful activity.

Bottom Lines (Self, Other, Work): These are three tasks that you will definitely do that day. If all else fails to get done, your bottom lines will be done.

Exercise, Nutrition, Rest: The components of energy are good food, rest, and exercise. Any time management system that you design should take care of you, too!

Ideas, Aha's: Your mind is the most powerful computer known and it is always plugged in. Ideas will come into the conscience part of your brain. At first glance, the idea might not apply to the urgent problems at hand. "Aha" means that you record these ideas because they frequently make sense later.

---

[3] Napolean Hill's idea for success, which is written about extensively in his books.

DATE	Day's Theme		Purpose		Nutrition	
			Planning		Rest	
			Preview		Exercise	
			Feared		Idea	
			Self		Mentor	
			Others		Review	
			Work		TOTAL	

Today's HOT List 20% activity			6am	
Feared			7am	
Self			8am	
Other				
Work			9am	
Exercise				
			10am	
			11am	
			12noon	
			1pm	

Today's 80% ACTIVITIES not-hot		2pm
		3pm
		4pm
		5pm
		6pm

Ideas/ Aha's	7pm
	Evening

Fig. 31.   Daily planner.

Mentor: Be a teacher, trainer, coach, or councilor to someone every day.

Review: Take an opportunity to review the events of the prior day. Pat yourself on the back where you did well, and review where you didn't. Look to improve your performance.

Total (Scoring System): The total is 13 points, but 10 is considered a perfect score. Shoot for 21 days of 10+ scoring.

Today's Hot List 20% Activity: These are the 20% (important, high return on investment) tasks that day. You will devote high-energy time to these activities. They include 8 items from the 13 that generate scoring. Concentrate on category 3, "Important—Not Urgent" items.

Today's 80% Activities Not-Hot (Bottom block of form): These are the nice-to-do tasks that you will do if you get a chance. They are not essential for your program.

Notes, Aha's: Space for notes and aha's.

Today's Plan: A schedule for the performance of the 20% activities; also a place to schedule meetings, calls, and other activity.

Descriptions of the Areas on page 2 (Fig. 32) of the Scheduling Sheets

Messages: In my case, these are telephone messages. I record the time and date that I pick up the messages. If I pick up messages a second or third time, I will write the new time.

20/80: I rate each call when I hear it. This rating sometimes changes. 20% is important, high return on investment activity. 80% is the low return on investment activity.

Notes: This is where I put in notes about a call or project.

Taming 20 Time Killers[4]

1. Take control of small parts of your day. Do not allow interruptions during these times; reroute calls to a crew member, clerk, or other supervisor. Use this time for bottom lines (high return on investment activity). Guard your high-energy times.

[4] Some of these items were based in part on an article entitled "Doing Time," which appeared in the February 1987 issue of *Microservice Management,* a magazine for people and companies that service microcomputers.

2. Some meetings are energy killers. Never schedule meetings during your high-energy times. The best time for meetings that you control are around lunch time and at the end of the day. The exception is the 15-minute "hit the ground running" meetings.

3. Train yourself to be able to throw things away and put things away. You may walk around a pile of magazines for months before realizing they can be put in the circular file. Look around your work space, and once a month throw some junk away. Do it until only current or important stuff is left. This is a good filler activity when you are low on energy or have a few extra minutes.

4. Get used to the fact that you don't have all of the answers. When something stumps you, restate the problem, and spend time trying to isolate the core of the problem. Seek out people with knowledge both inside and outside your firm. Focus on gathering information rather than looking for answers.

5. Attack your overweight bulging Rolodex. Business would screech to a halt without these phone number/business card organizers. As with many good things, a little is great but too much is not better. The goal is to have a slim Rolodex that is quick to use. Limit it to your current, most often-used numbers. File the cards that are not current or important right now. Develop a habit of writing the date on every Rolodex card. Make sure every number and address you use regularly is in your Rolodex. If you have a speed dialer, set it up now.

6. Put T.O. (throw out) dates on all files. These T.O. dates will keep your files clean. Every six months, review your files and throw away the old ones.

7. (Try this.) When a trade journal comes in, read the table of contents. Rip out the articles you want to read and put them in a reading file. This is an excellent file to help you take advantage of waiting time. This works for the newspaper. Try this after everyone else has seen it. Go through the paper, front to back, and circle the articles you want to read.

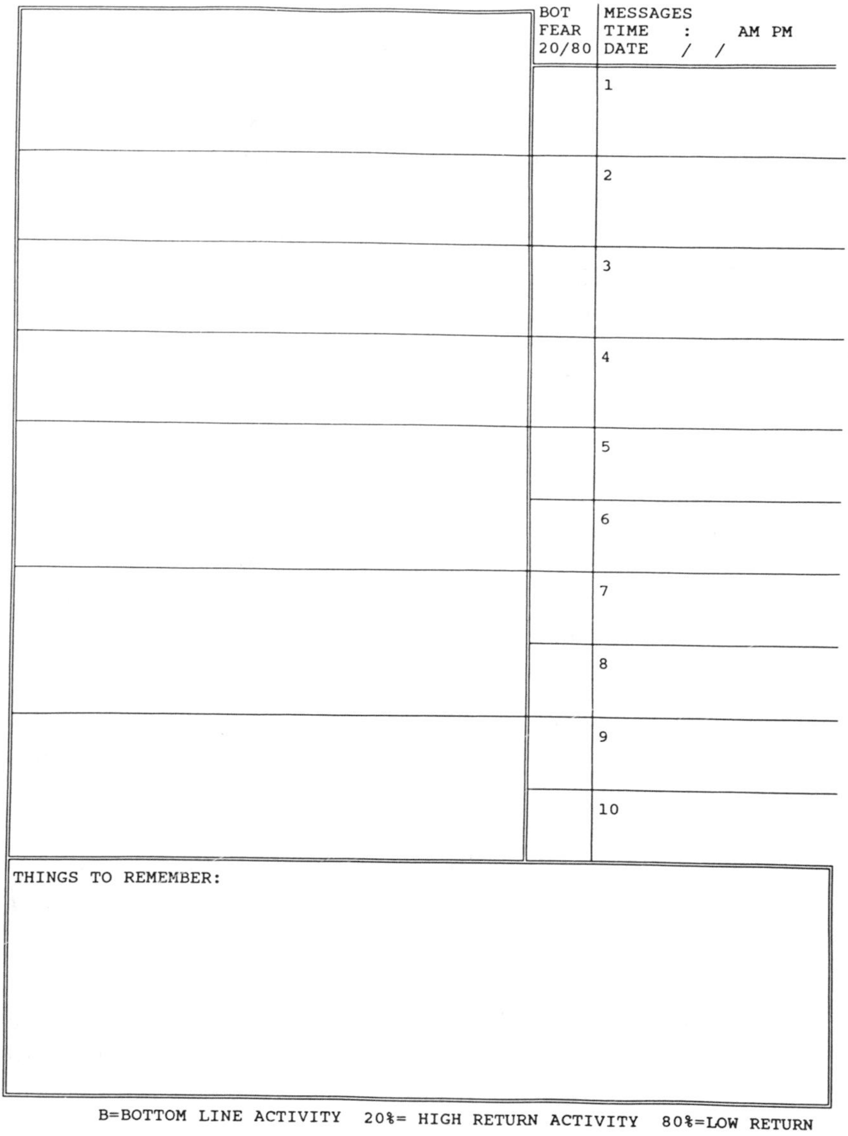

	BOT FEAR 20/80	MESSAGES TIME : AM PM DATE / /
		1
		2
		3
		4
		5
		6
		7
		8
		9
		10

THINGS TO REMEMBER:

B=BOTTOM LINE ACTIVITY   20%= HIGH RETURN ACTIVITY   80%=LOW RETURN

Fig. 32.   Messages.

Then go back and read the circled ones. You will find time savings.

8. Buy speed-listening equipment. Earlier we discussed getting cassette tapes and listening to them. The average brain can

process information faster than most people can talk. Firms have developed speed-listening tape players. These tape players speed up the tapes by skipping very short segments and playing the rest of the tape at normal speeds. The pitch of the speech and music is normal, but the elapsed time is variable up to $\frac{1}{2}$ of normal.

9. Know and drill yourself on doing jobs to an appropriate level of quality. For example, a punch press tool designed for millions of pieces will be made to a different quality standard than a temporary tool to make 15 pieces. Some of your projects need to be done "quick and dirty" and others need excellence. Know the difference. Inappropriate quality is a time killer.

10. Insist that people do their homework—it's the best way to get the best return on investment from meetings. The least efficient meeting is one where people sit around and watch each other think! Always schedule prep time for meetings that you attend.

11. If you feel overwhelmed with different projects, sit quietly for 1 or 2 minutes and allow worries to surface. List the worries that occur to you. The worries that occur first might be stopping you from the rest of your work. If possible, try to put the worry list to bed first.

12. After the worries are handled, decide on your most important jobs. This is called setting priorities. Do your highest priority or most anxiety-producing items early in the day.

13. Always work to complete what you start. Going back will always cost you time. Experts even extend this to reading the mail. Never pick up a piece of mail and put it down to deal with later. Pick it up once and deal with it.

14. Gain efficiency by grouping related activities together. For example, make all telephone calls together or assign all estimates to MWO's at the same time.

15. Divide larger projects into subprojects. This follows the philosophy of scheduling. Give yourself the extra motivation of allowing a completion (of a subproject) everyday.

16. Gain control of your own projects. Reverse load larger projects. Reverse loading starts with the completion date and works backward to the beginning of the project. This gives you logical subprojects and milestones to see if you are on schedule.

17. Use polite means to end telephone conversations that aren't going anywhere; for example: "Glad you called, but I have a meeting. Can I call you back?" Then call the person back at 4:50 P.M. to "chat."

18. Look at your junk mail. Ask yourself which types are useful. Have yourself removed from the useless lists (prepare a form postcard with "please remove my name from your list; I am no longer a prospect for your solicitations," tape their label to the postcard). Companies love to get these cards because it saves them money on wasted mailings.

19. There are several techniques to shorten meetings.

   • Have attendees stand up throughout.

   • Schedule them at 4:45 P.M. or 11:15 A.M. in the lunch room.

   • Try not to get invited if it doesn't concern you or your work group.

   • Have an agenda, and circulate the agenda to the attendees.

   • Stick to the agenda.

   • Start and end on time.

20. Do it now.

14.

Supervisor
Evaluation
Clinic

What Makes a Great Maintenance Supervisor?

We have discussed the issue of maintenance supervision with maintenance managers, maintenance supervisors, maintenance planners, plant engineers, building managers, and production managers throughout the United States and Canada. The organizations ranged from the largest industrial firms, federal and local governments, to small industrial and building management firms.[1] There were remarkable similarities in the answers between giant industrial firms and small firms, between the federal government and local agencies.

The following questions were asked about maintenance supervision:

1. What are the attributes of a good/great maintenance supervisor?

2. What is lacking in most supervisor training (if anything)?

[1] We would like to thank all the firms for their input in the form of discussions and questionnaires. Some of the firms that participated include (in alphabetical order): Amoco, AT&T, Baldor Electric, Bendix, Betz Laboratories, Bucks County Community College, City Service Oil, Clements Food, CSX, Cumberland Farms, Goodyear Tire, Honeywell Bell, IBM, IKEA, Indian Health Service, Johnson Controls, Kerr-McGee, OK Steel & Wire, Republic Gypsum, Rider College, Ross Laboratories, 3M, Texaco, Town of West Hartford, Trenton Housing Authority, Valley National Bank, Western Farmers Co-op, Wheatly Pump and Valve, and Xerox Corporation.

3. If you could give words of wisdom to a new supervisor what would they be?

The answers to these questions are discussed below.

What are the Attributes of a Good/Great Maintenance Supervisor?

We noticed that the answers fell into three general categories.

People Skills	Management Skills	Technical Skills
Good listener	Organized	Dedicated to quality
Compassionate	Able to make de-	Knows equipment
Can motivate	cisions	Knows job
others	Good delegator	Knows safety
Fair and con-	Meets goals of	Can analyze problems
sistent	business unit	Can evaluate skill
Respected	Able to re-analyze	level
Honest	progress to goal	Understands product
Effective trainer	Knows what is	
Open minded	and isn't im-	
Effective commu-	portant	
nicator	Provides good ser-	
A coach, not a	vice to cus-	
dictator	tomer	
Good negotiator	Loyal to organi-	
Has a cool head	zation	
Flexible	Oriented toward	
Can handle	results	
pressure	Good planner	
Can read people	High productivity	
Adaptable to	Follows up to see	
change	job is done	
Has common	Understands im-	
sense	portance of	
Willingness to	scheduling	
learn	Can assign and	
Positive outlook	keep priorities	

People Skills	Management Skills	Technical Skills
Innovative	Understands and	
Praises in public	uses budgets	
Disciplines in	Accessible	
private	Provides a con-	
Will take control	duit for down-	
if necessary	ward commu-	
Not afraid to	nication	
make mistakes	Provides intelli-	
Treats people as	gence to upper	
equals	management	
Can work with		
different types		
of people		
Gives recognition		
for job well		
done		
Can deal with dif-		
ficult people		
issues		

Notice that most of the comments from these managers centered around people and management skills.

What is Lacking in Most Supervisor Training (if Anything)?

We don't train our supervisors. They learn in the trenches.

Training in listening and communication.

We don't train them how to motivate, how to be a leader, or in psychology.

How to handle alcoholism, drug abuse, other employee problems.

Increased knowledge in allied fields (an electrical supervisor should know some plumbing or pneumatics).

Training in probable causes, results of actions/inaction.

How to deal with different types of people.

Ability to read people and know their limits.

How to supervise friends, older workers, young workers.

How to deal tactfully with inadequate performance issues.

How to work with budgets.

Use common sense.

How to keep personalities out of it; how to not impose lifestyle.

Administrative training.

Cost analysis.

The management of maintenance—the big picture.

Knowledge of how to use the organization's systems and procedures to get things done.

Some Gems of Wisdom to New Supervisors

Be a good listener.

Learn to bend, but don't abdicate.

Remember you are in charge, and act that way.

Strive to be respected, not necessarily liked.

Always be available to people.

Cultivate your patience. Know which things can be put off or ignored and which can't.

Pay attention to what people are saying.

Never stop learning.

Treat people consistently, fairly, and firmly.

Keep your eyes open—don't just look, *see.*

Make time to analyze your problem areas, and compile facts before deciding.

Those tough, humbling experiences are valuable, so treasure them.

Give clear indications of what a good job is, and give praise when it is achieved.

Don't be afraid to acknowledge that you don't know.

Quality cannot be ordered, it is an attitude.

There is a fine line between getting involved and getting in the way.

Good supervisors surround themselves with good people and are not afraid of training replacements.

Keep a positive attitude, and keep company interests at heart.

Set goals every day, and review them before leaving. Plan your days.

Listen more, talk less. Be able to hear feedback you don't like.

Solicit the views of the workers for improvements and problem areas.

Use positive, one-on-one techniques with workers.

Follow your work plan.

Keep records to back up your actions.

What is Your Personality Style?

We wanted to see what type of people were attracted to maintenance. We asked over 450 maintenance supervisors and managers to take a simple personality test. We used a self-administered version of a popular test called the Meyers-Briggs Personality Inventory. This test (which might be used by your Human Resources Department) divides personalities into four dimensions. Each dimension can be divided into two traits. You then score a series of questions and get a score in each trait. The higher the score, the more pronounced the trait.

The eight traits are: I (introverted), N (intuitive), T (thinker), P (perceiver), E (extroverted), S (senser), F (feeler), and J (judger).

Guidelines for the 8 Traits: The comment before each dimension is the broad category; the percentage after the category is percent occurrence in general population; the second percentage is the results of an analysis of the personalities of 450 maintenance supervisors.

I–E: How You Choose to Relate to the World, and Where You Focus Your Attention

I (Introverted): 25% in the general population, and 51% in the maintenance population. "I"-type person is likely to agree with the following statements.

I am reserved.

I like to puzzle out issues in my own mind first.

I prefer being alone or with one or two people I know well.

I communicate little of my inner thinking and feelings.

I tend to make decisions without consulting others.

I like quiet, thoughtful time alone.

People who are more introverted than extroverted tend to make decisions somewhat independently of constraints and prodding from the situation, culture, other people, or things around them. They are quiet and diligent at working alone, and socially reserved. They may dislike being interrupted while working. They also tend to forget names and faces. Maintenance departments also have personalities. If the Introverted trait predominates in the departments, then the style will be reserved, insulated, secretive, using little or no consultation with people outside the department, and may be misunderstood.

Possible Strengths	Possible Weaknesses
independent	misunderstands the external
works alone	avoids others
diligent	secretive
works with ideas	misunderstood by others
careful of generalizations	needs quiet to work
careful before acting	dislikes being interrupted

E (Extroverted): 75% in the general population, and 49% in the maintenance population. "E"-type people are likely to agree with the following statements.

I enjoy discussing a new, unconsidered issue at length in a group.

I prefer activities and occurrences in which others join.

I like talking freely for an extended period and thinking to myself at a later time.

I always try to make decisions after finding out what others think.

I like active, energetic time with people.

I enjoy meeting new people.

Extroverted people are attuned to the culture, people, and things around them, and they try to make decisions congruent with demands and expectations. The extrovert is outgoing, socially free, interested in variety and in working with people. The extrovert may become impatient with long, slow tasks, and does not mind being interrupted by people.

Possible Strengths	Possible Weaknesses
understands the external world	has less independence
interacts with others	does not work without
open	people

Possible Strengths	Possible Weaknesses
acts /does	needs change and variety
well understood	impulsive
	impatient with routine

N–S: How You See the World, How You Acquire Information

N (Intuitive): 25% in the general population, and 43% in the maintenance population. Likely to agree with the following statements.

It's fun to design plans and structures without necessarily carrying them out.

I like ideas.

I like the abstract or theoretical.

I enjoy thinking about possibilities.

I always try to think of new methods of doing tasks when confronted with them.

I am called imaginative or intuitive.

The intuitive person prefers possibilities, theories, the overall picture, invention, and the new, and becomes bored with nitty-gritty details, the concrete and actual, and facts unrelated to concepts. The intuitive person thinks and discusses in spontaneous leaps of intuition that may leave out or neglect details. Problem solving comes easily for this type of person, although there is a tendency to make errors of fact.

Possible Strengths	Possible Weaknesses
sees possibilities	inattentive to detail and
sees gestalts (holistic view)	precision

Possible Strengths	Possible Weaknesses
images and intuits	inattentive to the actual and
works out new ideas	practical
works with the complicated	impatient with the tedious
solves novel problems	leaves things our in leaps of
	logic
	loses sight of the here-and-now
	jumps to conslusions

S (Senser): 75% in the general population, and 57% in the maintenance population. Likely to agree with the following statements.

I like to carry out carefully laid, detailed plans with precision.

I want to know the factual details available.

I prefer the concrete or real.

I like to deal with actualities.

I like to use methods I know well that are effective to get the job done.

I am called factual and accurate.

The sensing type of person prefers the concrete, real, factual, structured, tangible, here-and-now, and becomes impatient with theory and the abstract, and mistrusts intuition. The sensing person thinks in careful detail, remembering real facts, making few errors of fact, but possibly missing a conception of the overall.

Possible Strengths	Possible Weaknesses
attends to detail	does not see possibilities
practical	loses the overall in the detail
has memory for fact	mistrusts intuition
works with tedious detail	does not work with the new
patient	frustrated with the complicated
careful, systematic	prefers not to imagine the future

F–T: Which Type of Decision Making is More Comfortable?

F (Feeler): 50% in the general population, and 47% in the maintenance population. Likely to agree with the following statements.

I enjoy experiencing emotional situations, discussions, movies.

I like people who show feelings.

I have convictions.

I use common sense and conviction to make decisions.

I enjoy helping others explore their feelings.

I like being thought of as a feeling person.

I come to conclusions based on what I feel and believe about life and people.

I make decisions about people in organizations based on empathy, feelings, and understanding of their needs and values.

The feeler makes judgments about life, people, occurrences, and things based on empathy, warmth, and personal values. As a consequence, feelers are more interested in people and feelings than in impersonal logic, analysis, and things, and in conciliation and harmony more than in being on top or achieving personal goals. The feeler gets along well with people.

Possible Strengths	Possible Weaknesses
considers other's feelings	not guided by logic; not
understands needs, values, feelings	objective
interested in conciliation	uncritical and overly
persuades, arouses	acccepting
	less organized
	bases justice on feelings

T (Thinker): 50% in the general population, and 52% in the maintenance population. Likely to agree with the following statements.

I like using my ability to analyze situations.

I prefer verifiable conclusions.

I like logical people.

I like being thought of as a thinking person.

I come to conclusions based on unemotional logic and careful step-by-step analysis.

I make decisions about people in organizations based on available data and systematic analysis of situations.

The thinker makes judgments about life, people, occurrences, and things based on logic, analysis, and evidence, avoiding the irrationality of making decisions based on feelings and values. As a result, the thinker is more interested in logic, analysis, and verifiable conclusions than in empathy, values, and personal warmth. The thinker may step on other people's feelings and needs without realizing it, neglecting to take into consideration the values of others.

Possible Strengths	Possible Weaknesses
logical, analytical	does not notice people's feelings
objective	misunderstands other's values
organized	uninterested in conciliation
has critical ability	does not show feelings
just	shows less mercy
stands firm	uninterested in persuading

P–J: How You Handle Time, and What Type of World You Prefer

P (Perceiver): 40% in the general population, and 22% in the maintenance population. Likely to agree with the following statements.

I like being free to do things on the spur of the moment.

I dislike using appointment books and notebooks.

I start meetings when all are comfortable or ready.

I believe in planning as necessities arise, just before carrying out the plan.

I like change and keeping options open.

I review every possible angle for a long time before and after making a decision.

I avoid making deadlines.

I allow commitments if others want to make them.

The perceiver is a gatherer, always wanting to know more before deciding, usually holding off decisions and judgments. As a consequence, the perceiver is open, flexible, adaptive, nonjudgmental, able to see and appreciate all sides of an issue, always welcoming new perspectives and new information about issues. However, perceivers are also difficult to pin down and may be indecisive and noncommittal, becoming involved in so many tasks that do not reach closure that they might become frustrated at times. Even when they finish tasks, perceivers will tend to look back at them and wonder whether they are satisfactory or could have been done another way. The perceiver wishes to accept life rather than change it.

Possible Strengths	Possible Weaknesses
compromises	indecisive
sees all sides of issues	does not plan
flexible and adaptable	has no order
remains open for change	does not control circumstances
decides based on all data	easily distracted from tasks
not judgmental	does not finish projects

J (Judger): 60% in the general population, and 78% in the maintenance population. Likely to agree with the following statements.

I like setting a schedule and sticking to it.

I get the information I need, consider it for a while, and then make a fairly quick, firm decision.

I plan ahead based on projections.

I keep appointments and notes about commitments in notebooks or appointment books as much as possible.

I prefer knowing well in advance what I am expected to do.

I tend to start meetings at a prearranged time.

The judger is decisive, firm, and sure—setting goals and sticking to them. The judger wants to close books, make decisions, and get on to the next project. When a project does not yet have closure, judgers want to leave it behind and go on to new tasks and not look back.

Possible Strengths	Possible Weaknesses
decides	unyielding, stubborn
plans	inflexible, unadaptable
orders	decides with insufficient data
controls	judgmental
makes quick decisions	controlled by task or plans
remains with a task	wishes not to interrupt work

Combinations[2]

NT: 12% in the general population and 19% in the maintenance population. Focuses on the abstract, analytical, new ideas applying logical processes; tends to be visual, visionary, competent, bookish, and sometimes arrogant.

NF: 12% in the general population and 24% in the maintenance population. Focuses on relationships and possibilities; likes new projects and new people; is an optimist; likes experiences; would make excellent journalists or coaches.

SJ: 38% in the general population and 44% in the maintenance population. Practical, organized, fair, consistent; uses rules and "shoulds."

---

[2] *Introduction to Type,* by Isbel Myers, published by Consulting Psychologists Press, Inc., 3803 E. Bayshore Rd., Palo Alto, CA 94303. This publisher owns the trademark for the test. Some of the descriptions of this and the next section are a partial adaption of the descriptions in this booklet. It also lists several good references for people who want to pursue the topic.

SP: 38% in the general population and 12% in the maintenance population. Spontaneous, flexible, a fire fighter, becomes immersed in tasks; good at crafts.

Description of the 16 Personality Combinations, and Their Frequency in the Maintenance Population

ISTJ (14.5%): These individuals are well organized, serious, quiet, and have a respect for and facility with facts. On the surface, they are calm in crisis, but might have a strong reaction underneath. They take responsibility, and will make up their own minds about a situation and work slowly/methodically regardless of protests or distractions. They tend to stabilize projects and work-groups. They are at risk of thinking that everyone is like them, and of overriding less forceful people. They might also minimize imagination and intuition.

ESTJ (13.8%): Individuals with this combination are very organized and like to set goals. They will be a practical maintenance person who is realistic and matter of fact—more interested in here-and-now—a naturally good mechanic. They like to organize and run things using logical processes. They can be a natural maintenance supervisor when they can consider other's feelings and values; although they may decide too quickly.

INFJ (10.2%): These supervisors will succeed through perseverance and originality. They are strong "idea" people driven by inspirations. They should take care to avoid being smothered by routine aspects of job. They put best efforts into work; quietly forceful, conscientious, and concerned about others, and respected for firm principles. They desire to do what is needed or wanted. However, they must temper inspirations with development of their thought process.

ENTJ (10%): These individuals are hearty, frank, decisive, well-informed leaders, who enjoy long-range planning and thinking ahead. They are good at logical, intelligent, reasonable speaking. Their main interest is in seeing possibilities beyond the present, though they may be overoptimistic for the situation. They need someone around with common sense, because they may decide too quickly and may ignore other people's values and feelings.

ENFJ (8.5%): These supervisors are sociable, popular, and responsive to both praise and criticism. They are persevering, orderly, conscientious and interested in possibilities and harmony. They are concerned about what others think, want, and feel, so can present proposals or facilitate groups with ease and tact. Might tend to jump to conclusions. They have many rules, "shoulds," and "should-nots."

ESFJ (8.1%): This describes a warm-hearted outgoing maintenance supervisor who is a born cooperator. He or she has little interest in technical areas. This person will create harmony and find value in other people's opinions, and is practical, orderly, and down to earth, works best in a warm encouraging, supportive environment. This individual has a lot of "shoulds," rules, and assumptions about situations.

ISFJ (7.9%): These are quiet, friendly, responsive, and dependable supervisors who will work devotedly to meet an obligation. They will lend a stable influence to any team, and care about the people on their crews. They are thorough and painstakingly accurate. May need time to master technical areas. They are at risk of becoming withdrawn. Also, they do not trust imagination and intuition.

INTJ (4.2%): This combination makes for maintenance supervisors with original minds, great ideas, strong intuition, and the power to organize and carry out jobs with or without help. They will drive others as strongly as themselves. They are also considered stubborn, skeptical, and independent; they are single-minded and should seek (and need) the input of others to balance them. They need to develop their thinking so that they can evaluate their own inspirations.

ISFP (4%): These people are quiet, friendly, sensitive, and modest. They might not show warmth until they know you well. They look at the world through their own deeply held values. They don't like disagreements. They are craft oriented, loyal followers, and do not usually choose to lead. They like a slow pace. They might not measure up to inner ideals and may feel inadequate.

ESFP (3.6%): These supervisors are outgoing, easy-going, accepting, and friendly. They are very flexible problem-solvers, not bound by current rules and procedures; actively curious about people, objects, food, or anything sensory. They know what is going on through the grapevine (and participate). They remember facts better than theory and learn by doing due to good common sense.

They might be too easy on discipline and their love for a good time might put them at risk.

INTP (3.6%): These quiet maintenance supervisors are extremely logical, abstract, interested in ideas, and have sharply defined interests. They are more interested in ideas than the practical application of the ideas in the world. They have little need for social small-talk, get-togethers, and anything else not in their area of interest. They might overlook other people's values and feelings.

INFP (3.4%): These enthusiastic maintenance supervisors are not very concerned with surroundings or trappings. They are deeply driven by inner convictions that are usually difficult to express. They enjoy learning, ideas, languages, and independent projects, and can be very absorbed in current activity. Sometimes they are excellent writers. They're not usually talkative until they know you well. Some may feel they don't measure up to their inner standards.

ISTP (3.2%): These cool, quiet, reserved supervisors analyze everything with detachment. They prefer to organize ideas and facts rather than people or situations, and so are interested in impersonal principles and why mechanical things work. They could have great capacity to understand the facts of a situation, and are engineering oriented. They will not overexert themselves, may overlook other people's needs and values, and may not follow through.

ENTP (1.7%): These individuals are quick, ingenious, energetic, and good at many things. Their thinking helps temper their intuition, and they might neglect routine assignments. They're resourceful at new, unique, novel problems. They are stimulating company, and might argue either side of an issue for fun. They must constantly feel challenged. They need to learn to follow through; without development of their judgment, they will waste their energy on ill-chosen projects.

ENFP (1.5%): These are warm, enthusiastic maintenance supervisors, with a can-do attitude, they see possibility everywhere. They are quick to help and offer solutions. They are skillful people-handlers with great insight. They will improvise rather than plan in advance—they hate routine. They might leave projects after the core problems are solved. They become bored and leave projects incomplete.

ESTP (1.2%): These people are no-worry no-hurry supervisors. They operate from concrete reality—what they can see, hear, touch, taste, or smell. They enjoy sensory pleasures. They are not bound by current rules and procedures to find the solutions to problems. They like mechanical things and movement. They are blunt and occasionally insensitive. They will be a natural craftsperson when they can include people. Even after they are supervisors, they keep a mechanical hobby at home for the joy of it. Their love of a good time might be a risk.

Hints in Applying the Inventory to Individual Situations

1. People who have the same strengths in the dimensions seem to click together; they arrive at decisions more quickly. They seem to operate on the same wavelength. They work from similar assumptions.

2. Different traits have different strengths, i.e., the intuitive is best at seeing the future; the sensor sees practical realism; the thinker uses analysis; and the feeler is adept at handling people.

3. The problem with people who have the same strengths in the dimensions is blind spots. Their decisions may suffer because they have similar weaknesses.

4. People with different strengths may not see eye to eye on many things. The more the group differs, the more likely misunderstanding and conflict will occur.

5. The advantage of groups with different strengths is that decisions may be improved as a result of the differing points of view.

6. People might be sensitive about criticism in their areas of weakness. These people might avoid using their weaker sides, and conflict might occur when they must use those dimensions or when others point out deficiencies.

7. A person's makeup cannot be changed to its opposite. Each person can realize where their weaknesses lie and work to strengthen them.

8. People's values, beliefs, decisions, and actions will be profoundly influenced by all four of their stronger dimensions.

9. Groups with a preponderance of members with similar strengths should seek out and listen to other types when making decisions. This is essential for major decisions.

10. If you want to look into this test as a team-building tool, contact your Human Resources Department and ask for the Meyers-Briggs Personality Inventory. They should have copies and information on its use.

Glossary of Maintenance Management Terms

Asset: Either a machine, building, or system. It is the basic unit of maintenance.

Autonomous maintenance: Routine maintenance and PM's are carried out by operators in independent groups. These groups, which may include maintenance workers, solve problems without management intervention. The maintenance department is only officially called for bigger problems that require more resources, technology, or downtime.

Backlog: All work available to be done. Backlog work has been approved, parts are either listed or bought, and everything is ready to go.

BNF equipment: Equipment left off of the PM system, left in the *Bust 'N Fix* mode (it busts and you fix—no PM at all).

Call back: Job where the maintenance person is called back because the asset broke again or the job wasn't finished the first time. (See **Rework.**)

Capital spares: Usually large, expensive, long-leadtime parts that are capitalized (not expensed) on the books and depreciated. They are protection against downtime.

Certificate of insurance: A document from the insurance company that verifies insurance coverage for contractors on larger jobs. It will have dates that coverage is in effect, and the dollar limits and types of the coverage.

Charge-back: Maintenance work that is charged to the user. All work orders should be costed and billed back to the user's department. The maintenance budget is then included with the user budgets. Also called rebilling.

Charge rate: This is the rate in dollars that you charge for a mechanic's time. In addition to the direct wages, you add benefits and overhead (such as supervision, clerical support, shop tools, truck expenses, supplies). You might pay a tradesperson $15/hr and use a $35/hr (or greater) charge rate.

CM: See **Corrective maintenance.**

Computerphobia: Irrational fear or dread of computers.

Continuous improvement: Reduction to the inputs (hours, materials, management time) to maintenance to provide a given level of maintenance service. Increases in the number of assets, or use of assets with fixed or decreasing inputs.

Core damage: When a normally rebuildable component is damaged so badly that it cannot be repaired.

Corrective maintenance (CM): Maintenance activity that restores an asset to a preserved condition. Normally initiated as a result of a scheduled inspection. (See **Scheduled work.**)

Deferred maintenance: This is all of the work you know needs to be done that you choose not to do. You put it off, usually in hope of retiring the asset or getting authorization to do a major job that will include the deferred items.

DIN work: "Do It Now" means nonemergency work that you have to do now. An example would be moving furniture in the executive wing.

Emergency work: Maintenance work requiring immediate response from the maintenance staff. Usually associated with some kind of danger, safety, damage, or major production problems.

FAS: Shipping term meaning Free Along Side (you are responsible for the loading charge), commonly used for ships or very large freight.

Feedback: When used in the maintenance PM sense, feedback means information from your individual failure history is accounted for in the task list. The list is increased in depth or frequency when failure history is high, the list is decreased when failure history is low.

FOB (City, Shipping point, or Delivered): Free On Board (seller will load truck or rail car). The FOB point is important because of both the responsibility for the shipment and the freight charges. "FOB delivered" keeps the vendor responsible for the shipment until it reaches your door. "FOB shipping point" or "FOB originating city" makes you responsible for the shipment. If there is a problem with an FOB originating city shipment, you still have to pay the vendor and file a claim with the carrier.

Frequency of inspection: How often do you do the inspections? What criteria do you use to initiate the inspection? (See **PM clock.**)

Future benefit PM: PM task lists that are initiated by a breakdown rather than a usual schedule. The PM is done on a whole machine, assembly line, or process after a section or subsection breaks down. This is a popular method with manufacturing cells where the individual machines are closely coupled. When one machine breaks, then the whole cell is PM'ed.

GLO: Generalized Learning Objective means the general items necessary to know to be successful in a job. Each job description would be made up of a series of GLO's.

Iatrogenic: Failures that are caused by your own service person.

IBM® compatible: A personal computer that follows the rules of the IBM®-type machine. The rules include type of microprocessor chip, setup of internal wiring, ways to communicate, and others. All of the software examples in this text are based on this standard. It is also the most common standard in business. The other standard is based on the Apple Macintosh®. Many of the programs are also available for Apple systems.

In-bin work: Maintenance jobs which are not ready to release to the mechanic because you haven't approved or gotten money, parts are on order and not in, or other problem.

Inspection list: See **Task list.**

Inspectors: The special crew or special role that has primary responsibility for PM's. Inspectors can be members of the maintenance department or of any other department (machine operators, drivers, security officers, custodians, etc.).

Interruptive (task): Any PM task which interrupts the normal operation of a machine, system, or asset.

Labor: Physical effort a person has to expend to repair, inspect, or deal with a problem. It is expressed in hours, and can be divided by crafts or skills.

Life cycle: This denotes the stage in life of the asset. Three stages are recognized by the author: startup, wealth, breakdown.

Life cycle cost (LCC): A total of all costs throughout all of the life cycles. Costs should include PM, repair (labor, parts, and supplies), downtime, energy, ownership, overhead. An adjustment can be made for the time value of money.

Log sheet: A document where you make log entry of all small jobs or short repairs.

MTBF: Mean Time Between Failures. Important calculation to help set up PM schedules and to determine reliability of a system.

MTTR: Mean Time To Repair. This calculation helps determine the cost of a typical failure. It also can be used to track skill level, training effectiveness, and effectiveness of maintenance improvements.

Maintainability improvement: Also called maintenance improvement. Maintenance engineering activity that looks at the root cause of breakdowns and maintenance problems and designs a repair that prevents breakdowns in the future. Also includes improvements to make the equipment more easily maintained.

Maintenance: The dictionary definition is "the act of holding or keeping in a preserved state." The dictionary doesn't say anything about repairs. It presumes that we are acting in such a way to avoid the failure by preserving the asset.

Maintenance prevention: Maintenance-free designs resulting from increased effectiveness in the initial design of the equipment.

Management: The act of controlling or handling.

Meter master: Form designed to record meter readings. There is also space for the subtraction for usage calculations.

MSDS: Material Safety Data Sheets. These sheets should come with any chemicals that you purchase. They give the formal name of the chemical, describe its toxicity, and have warnings on use. One master copy should be kept in the maintenance technical library.

Noninterruptive task list: PM task list where all of the tasks can safely be done without interrupting production of the machine.

Nonscheduled work: Work that you didn't know about and plan for at least the day before. Work falls into three categories: 1) emergency, 2) DIN, 3) routine.

Parts: All of the supplies, machine parts, and materials to repair an asset, or a system in or around an asset.

PCR: Planned Component Replacement. Maintenance schedules component replacement to a schedule based on MTBF, downtime costs, and other factors. Technique for ultrahigh reliability favored by the aircraft industry.

Pending work: Work that has been issued to a mechanic or contractor that is unfinished. It is important to complete all pending work.

Planned maintenance: See **Scheduled work.**

PM: Preventive Maintenance is a series of tasks that either extend the life of an asset, or that detect that an asset has had critical wear and is going to fail or break down.

PM clock: The parameter that initiates the PM task list for scheduling; usually buildings and assets in regular use (for example, PM every 90 days). Assets used irregularly may use other production measures such as pieces, machine hours, or cycles.

PM frequency: How often the PM task list will be done. The frequency is driven by the PM clock. (See **Frequency of inspection.**)

Predictive maintenance: Maintenance techniques that inspect an asset to predict if a failure will occur. For example, an infrared survey might be done of an electrical distribution system looking for hot spots (which would be likely to fail). In industry, predictive maintenance is usually associated with advanced technology such as infrared or vibration analysis.

Priority: The relative importance of the job. A safety problem would come before an energy improvement job.

Proactive: Action before a stimulus (opposite of reactive). A proactive maintenance department acts before a breakdown.

Reason for write-up (also called reason for repair): Why the work order was initiated. Reasons could include PM activity, capital improvements, breakdown, vandalism, and any others needed in that industry.

Rework: All work that has to be done over. Rework is bad and indicates a problem in materials, skills, or scope of the original job. (See **Call back.**)

RM: Replacement/Rehabilitation/Remodel Maintenance. All activity designed to bring an asset back into good shape, upgrade an asset to current technology, or make an asset more efficient/productive.

Root cause (root cause analysis): The root cause is the underlying cause of a problem. For example, you can snake out an old cast or galvanized sewer line every month and never be confident that it will stay open. The root cause is the hardened buildup inside the pipes which necessitates pipe replacement. Analysis would study the slow drainage problem and determine what was wrong and also estimate the cost of leaving it in place. Some problems (not usually this type of example) should not be fixed. Root cause analysis will show this.

Route maintenance: Mechanic has an established route through your facility to fix all the little problems reported to them. The route mechanic is usually very well equipped so he/she can deal with most small problems. Route maintenance and PM activity are sometimes combined.

Routine work: Work that is done on a routine basis where the work and material content is well known and understood, for example, daily line startups.

Scheduled work: Work that is written up by an inspector and known about at least 1 day in advance. The scheduler will put the work into the schedule to be done. Sometimes the inspector finds work that must be done immediately which becomes emergency or DIN. Same as planned maintenance or corrective maintenance.

Short repairs: Repairs that a PM or route person can do in less than 30 minutes with the tools and materials that he/she carries.

SLO: Specific Learning Objective is the detailed knowledge, skill, or attitude necessary to be able to do a job.

SM: Seasonal Maintenance. All maintenance activities that are related to time of year or time in business cycle. Cleaning roof drains of leaves after the autumn would be a seasonal demand. A swimming pool chemical company might have some November activities to prepare for the next season.

String-based PM: Usually simple PM tasks that are strung together on several machines. Examples of string PM's would include lubrication, filter change, or vibration routes.

Survey: A formal look around. All of the aspects of the facility are recorded and defined. The survey will look at every machine, room, and throughout the grounds. The surveyor will note anything that looks like it needs work.

SWO: Standing Work Order; work order for routine work. A standing work order will stay open for a week, month, or more. The

SWO for daily furnace inspection might stay open for a whole month.

Task: One line on a task list (see below) that gives the inspector specific instruction to do one thing.

Task list: Directions to the inspector about what to look for during that inspection. Tasks could be to inspect, clean, tighten, adjust, lubricate, replace, etc.

Technical library (Maintenance Technical Library): The repository of all maintenance information including (but only limited by your creativity and space) maintenance manuals, drawings, old notes on the asset, repair history, vendor catalogs, MSDS, PM information, engineering books, shop manuals, etc.

Terotechnology: "A combination of management, financial, engineering, and other practices applied to physical assets in pursuit of economic life-cycle costs (LCC). Its practice is concerned with specification and design for reliability and maintainability of plant machinery, equipment, buildings, and structures with their installation, commissioning, maintenance, modification, and replacement, and with feedback of information on design, performance, and costs" (from the definition endorsed by the British Standards Institute).

TPM: Total Productive Maintenance. A maintenance system set up to eliminate all of the barriers to production. It uses autonomous maintenance teams to carry out most maintenance activity.

UM: User Maintenance. This is any maintenance request primarily driven by a user. It includes breakdown, routine requests, and DIN jobs.

Unit: The asset that the task list is written for in a PM system. The unit can be a machine, a system, or even a component of a large machine.

Work order: Written authorization to proceed with a repair or other activity to preserve a building or asset.

Work request: Formal request to have work done. Can be filled out by an inspector during an inspection on a write-up form or by a maintenance user. Work requests are usually time/date stamped.

Resources

Magazines and Newsletters

Bits and Pieces Magazine, Economics Press, 12 Daniel Rd., Fairfield, NJ 07004-9987; phone: 800-526-2554. This diminutive booklet is filled with bits (and pieces) of common sense and wisdom. A great booklet to give to new and aspiring supervisors. It is published 26 times per year. Single issues cost about $30/year; $20/yr/copy for 50 copies of each issue.

Maintenance Supervisor's Bulletin, published twice monthly, is a newsletter with articles on all topics related to maintenance. Published by Bureau of Business Practice, Paramount Publishing Business Technical and Professional Group, 24 Rope Ferry Rd, Waterford, CT 06386-0001; phone: 800-243-0876, ext. 52.

Maintenance Technology, Applied Technology Publications, 1300 S. Grove Ave., Barrington, IL 60010. This is an excellent newcomer to the field that concentrates on the technology side of our businesses. Free.

Plant Engineering, Cahners Publications, Cahners Plaza, 1350 E. Touchy Ave., P.O. 5080, Des Plaines, IL 60017-5080. The best all-around journal. Free.

P/PM Technology, P/PM Technology, P.O. Box 9773, Truckee, CA 95737. A magazine dedicated to preventive and predictive maintenance. $36/yr. Excellent reprint service. Good source of background information on technology.

Practical Supervision, a monthly newsletter from Professional Training Associates, 210 Commerce Blvd., Round Rock, TX 78664; phone: 800-424-2112, Fax: 512-255-7532. This is specific training for supervisors and potential supervisors. It contains basic material for the new supervisor. $50/yr.

Associations

AMA (American Management Association), 135 West 50th St., New York, NY 10020. Seminars, books, and meetings about all facets of management.

American Institute of Plant Engineers (AIPE), 3975 Erie Ave., Cincinnati, OH 45208; phone: 513-561-6000. One of the more active associations for building engineers. They have extensive education opportunities. Be sure to get a copy of the Facilities Management library—a list of 75 books for sale on building maintenance management.

ATA (American Trucking Association), 2200 Mill Road, Alexandria, VA 22314. ATA is known for the VMRS (Vehicle Maintenance Reporting Standards), an excellent beginning to understand computerizing maintenance. Company membership starts at under $300/year.

Association of Energy Engineers, 4025 Pleasantdale Rd., Suite 420, Altanta, GA 30340; phone: 404-925-9558, Fax: 404-381-9865; Order Dept.: 588, P.O. Box 1026, Lilburn, GA 30226. Texts available on all building systems that supply or consume (lighting, chillers, cooling towers, HVAC, pumps, EMS, etc.) energy. Other topics include energy audits, governmental policy, and engineering reference texts.

Instrument Society of America. This association has developed interactive videos on systematic methods in troubleshooting. Each video contains 4–6 hours of instruction. Contact **Maintenance Technology** (listed under "Vendors.")

International Maintenance Institute, P.O. 266695, Houston, TX 77207. This organization is dedicated to furthering the goals of maintenance professionals. Dues are $25.

Roofing Industry Education Institute, 14 Inverness Dr. East, Bldg H, Suite 110, Englewood, CO 80112; phone: 303-790-7200. This is one of many associations that offer training. Their courses include Reroofing and Retrofit (3-day, $595), and Roof Inspection, Diagonsis, and Repair (2-day, $395).

Books

If You Haven't Got Time to Do It Right, When Will You Find Time to Do It Over? by Jeffery Mayer, published by Simon and Schuster, New York. This short, snappy book has excellent ideas for the harried supervisor.

The Management of Time, by James McCay, published by Prentice-Hall, Englewood Cliffs, NJ. This is an older book (first published in 1959) with some very relevant and up-to-date ideas. One of the great concepts is the quotation (that starts Chapter 2) from Lynn White, Jr.: "We live in an era when rapid change breeds fear, and fear too often congeals us into a rigidity which we mistake for stability."

One Page Management, by Riaz Khadem and Robert Lorber, published by William Morrow, New York. This book is part of the One Minute Management library promised by Ken Blanchard and Spencer Johnson a decade ago. All of these books have a common thread relating good time management to effective supervision. This book, in particular, speaks to the issue of paperwork and reporting (a major issue of supervision).

The Ninety Minute Hour, by Jay Conrad Levinson, published by E. P. Dutton, New York. Jay Levinson is an excellent author who, judging from the quality of his work, must practice what he preaches. This book highlights how to squeeze more productivity out of each hour. In my view, these ideas are essential to success.

The One Minute Manager, by Ken Blanchard and Spencer Johnson, published by Berkley Books, New York. This is the book that the section in Module 3 was based on. It takes about 2 hours to read, and it's worth it! These techniques are very effective and surprisingly easy to follow.

The Book of Five Rings, by Miyamoto Musashi, published by Bantam Books, New York. If you are interested in the Japanese view on business and business strategy, this is a translation of a 16th-century book on swordsmanship used in Japan today to train new managers. We will need the resolve and willpower described in this book to effectively compete in the future.

Handbook of Building Maintenance Management, by Mel A. Shear, published by Reston Publishing Co. (a Prentice-Hall Company), Reston, VA 22090 (TH3361.S45). This is a nuts-and-bolts book of building management. It combines ideas on the management of maintenance with the doing of maintenance. Excellent for maintenance departments that support the facility in addition to the equipment.

The Complete Handbook of Maintenance Management, by John E. Heintzelman, published by Prentice-Hall, Englewood Cliffs, NJ (TS192.H44). This is a very readable overview of the maintenance field.

Maintenance Management, by Jay Butler, available from Butler (see address in the "People" section). This book has been used to train 10,000 maintenance managers in the U.S., Canada, and the U.K.

Maintenance Management, by Don Nyman, available from USC, 100 State Street, 4th Floor, Boston, MA 02110. This text is a summary of maintenance lore and information from Don's 30 years as a top-level consultant. Includes an excellent questionnaire to evaluate your department.

Introduction to TPM, by Seiichi Nakajima, published by Productivity Press, P.O. Box 3007, Cambridge, MA 02140; phone: 617-497-5146. This book gives a complete overview of TPM. This book and its companion volume (below) are essential reading to understand TPM.

Total Productive Maintenance, An American Approach, by Terry Wireman, published by Industrial Press, 200 Madison Ave., New York, NY 10016. This book explains the steps for TPM for an American organization. It has many excellent ideas for organizations considering TPM.

TPM Development Program, by Seiichi Nakajima, published by Productivity Press, P.O. Box 3007, Cambridge, MA 02140; phone: 617-497-5146. This book gives a complete systems design to the set up and day-to-day working of a TPM system.

Computer Software

Formtool Gold Version 3.0, Bloc Publishing, 800 SW 37th Ave., Suite 765, Coral Gables, FL 33134. Some of the forms in this text are designed on form tool. This package is available at any computer store.

Pack Rat, Polaris Software, 17150 Via Del Campo Suite 307, San Diego, CA 92127; phone: 619-674-6500. This is one of the best of a new breed of software called PIM's (personal information managers). It is very flexible, and takes some time to learn. It can completely organize even a complex life! Useful for scheduled PM-type maintenance, project management, and resource scheduling.

PC-SIG (Special Interest Group), 1030D East Duane Ave., Sunnyvale, CA 94086. This is the national user group for personal computers. The major advantage of PC-SIG is their catalog of shareware software. It lists 2000 or more packages available for $10–$135.

People

You may want to attend training sessions offered by these individuals.

Butler, Jay, 5 North Branch River Road, Somerville, NJ is an expert trainer and consultant in maintenance management. His special expertise is in computerization and application of predicative maintenance.

Christian, Philip, P.O. Box 780, Alpharetta, GA 30201 is an expert in maintenance of grounds. His knowledge is used to reduce costs at universities, airports, and transit systems throughout the country. If your concern is grounds, seek him out.

Feldman, Edwin, P.O. Box 52729 Atlanta, GA 30355 (for list of books) has written several useful books about property maintenance and cleaning. Much of what he recommends applies to factories, too!

Guintini, Ronald, 1310 Hooper Ave., Toms River, NJ 08753 is one of the leading experts in maintenance inventory and accounting.

Nyman, Don, 67 Toppin Drive, Moss Creek Plantation, Hilton Head Island, SC 29926 is one of the leading experts in maintenance management and leads seminars for Clemson University and others.

Wireman, Terry, P.O. Box 550, Inkom, ID 83245 is the resident guru in TPM for many organizations. He also teaches maintenance management courses for several universities.

Organizations that Publish Cassette Courses

Crisp Publications, 95 First St., Los Altos, CA 94022; phone: 405-949-4888, Fax: 415-949-1610. The Crisp catalog offers a wide variety of books, cassettes, and videos. Topics run the gamut from time management to business writing, with 30 or 40 topics in between. Prices range from under $10 for books and cassettes to several hundred dollars for videos.

FlipTrack Learning Systems, 999 N. Main St., Dept. 191, Glen Ellyn, IL 60137; phone: 800-222-3547, Fax: 708-790-1196. One of the many good training tools for computer expertise. Their audio training covers most major PC software. Includes a course guide. Prices range from $100 to $200 per course.

Listen USA, 60 Arch St., Greenwich, CT 06830 interviews top business managers on their theories of management. Cost $7.95 to $12.50.

MW Corporation, One Croton-Point Avenue, Croton-on-Hudson, NY 10520; phone: 914-271-6658. This organization specializes in up-to-date team building seminars and tapes. If your manufacturing group is moving toward a continuous improvement process, see how maintenance can fit in.

National Seminars, 6901 West 63rd St., Shawnee Mission, KS 66202-4007; Fax: 913-432-0824. Some videos of interest to supervisors: "How to Supervise People," "Time Management," "How to Get Things Done;" $59.95 each. Also about 100 other tapes and books. I used some of "How to Get Things Done" in Chapter 13.

Nightengale-Conant Corp., 7300 North Lehigh Ave., Chicago, IL 60648; phone: 800-323-5552. This is probably the best company in the business of self-improvement cassettes. The topics range from improve your selling skills to their monthly cassette magazine *Insight*.

Simon and Schuster, P.O. Box 10212, Des Moines, IA 50381; phone: 800-678-2677. This is a good source for low-cost tapes to listen to on your commutes to work or for field service calls. Costs run $7.95 and up; topics range from current business books to self-help to mysteries.

Springfield Resources, 902 Oak Lane Ave., Philadelphia, PA 19126-3336; phone: 215-924-0270. This company specializes in maintenance management training. It markets several audiotaped courses by the author in general maintenance, maintenance supervision, and industry-specific maintenance.

Vendors of Maintenance Information/Training

American Technical Publishers, 1155 West 175th St. Homewood, IL 60430; phone: 800-323-3471. A great source for trade training. This includes books for carpenters, electricians, and plumbers. Prices range from $10 to $50, with most of the offerings under $20.

Applied Learning Corp., Industrial Learning Division, 1751 West Diehl Rd., Naperville, IL 60563-9099; phone: 800-323-0377, fax and voice: 708-369-3000. Their catalog reads more like a phone book than a course catalog, with over 2000 offerings. The two areas that caught my eye were hundreds of courses in shop disciplines and hundreds more in computerization. Courses are available in interactive video, booklet, and in several languages.

Baker Instrument Co., Box 587, Ft. Collins, CO 80522; phone: 303-221-3150, Fax: 303-221-3013. Baker is a vendor of test instruments. They produce a seminar titled "Keep Your Motors Running," concerning electrical testing for reliability and predictive maintenance.

Bruel & Kjaer, 1140 Bloomfield Ave., West Caldwell, NJ 07006; phone: 201-227-6100. This instrument company is one of the leading companies in the vibration analysis field. They put on a series of seminars on vibration measurement and analysis throughout the year. The cost is $125 per day (an excellent value).

Clemson University, College of Commerce and Industry, Office of Professional Development, P.O. Drawer 921, Clemson, SC 29633-0912. Clemson has a national program in maintenance management training with several excellent instructors. They visit almost every region on a periodic basis.

Concordia, Center for Management Studies, 1550 Maisonneuve Blvd. W, Suite 403, Montreal, P.Q., HSG 1N2, Canada. Offers maintenance management seminars in both French and English.

Industrial Press, 200 Madison Ave., New York, NY 10016. In addition to publishing the popular *Machinery's Handbook,* they publish several good maintenance management texts.

Lion Technology Inc., P.O. Drawer 700, Lafayette, NJ 07848; phone: 201-383-0800, Fax: 201-579-6818. Lion is one of the leading firms in the area of training workshops on hazardous/toxic waste management; their popular 2-day workshop is listed at $600.

Maintenance Technology, 1300 South Grove Ave., Suite 205, Barrington, IL 60010; phone: 800-223-3423, Fax: 708-304-8603. *Maintenance Technology* is one of the best maintenance magazines. They have developed a troubleshooting course complete with a hands on troubleshooting platform. Their system includes workbooks and an administrator's guide.

General Physics Corp. (contact **Maintenance Technology**) provides training services with over 250 courses in electrical, electronics, instrumentation, mechanical, and manufacturing.

National Technology Transfer, P.O. Box 110397, Aurora, CO 80042-0397; phone: 800-922-2820. This firm travels around the country and gives classes on important maintenance topics using unique fixtures with actual devices (hydraulic systems, PLC's, etc.) built in; this is an excellent training modality.

Pacific Lutheran University, Center for Executive Development, Tacoma, WA 98447. PLU has an excellent continuing education department that sponsors a variety of maintenance courses in Seattle throughout the year.

Ramsey Corp., Boyce Station Offices, 1050 Boyce Road, Pittsburgh, PA 15241-3907; phone: 412-257-0732. This company designs and administers maintenance tests in all crafts. We believe that it is essential to determine competency before training is prescribed.

Rowan College, Management Institute, 201 Mullica Hill Road, Glassboro, NJ 08028. Rowan gives a certificate in maintenance management. They schedule courses in the Cherry Hill, NJ, area twice a year.

Springfield Resources, 902 Oak Lane Ave., Philadelphia, PA 19126-3336; phone: 215-924-0270. This company specializes in maintenance management training. It can deliver on-site training in several topics, including general maintcnance, maintenance supervision, and industry-specific maintenance.

TPC Training Systems, 750 Lake Creek Rd., Buffalo Grove, IL 60089; phone: 708-808-4000. TPC is a craft training company. The courses consist of programmed learning texts, teacher's guide, and audio visuals. Some courses are available in Spanish.

University of Alabama, Professional and Management Development Programs, Box 870388, Tuscaloosa, AL 35487-0388. UOA has one of the best conference centers in the whole South. They offer a wide range of courses for professional and management development.

Index

Index